OUTSPOKEN

OUTSPOKEN

OUTSPOKEN

OUTSPOKEN

OUTSPOKEN

OUTSPOKEN

OUTSPOKEN

OUTSPOKEN

OUTSPOKEN

OUTSPOKEN
OUTSPOKEN
OUTSPOKEN

WHY WOMEN'S VOICES GET SILENCED AND HOW TO SET THEM FREE

VERONICA RUECKERT

**HARPER
BUSINESS**

An Imprint of HarperCollins*Publishers*

HarperCollins books may be purchased for educational, business, or sales promotional use. For information, please email the Special Markets Department at SPsales@harpercollins.com.

FIRST EDITION

Designed by Leah Carlson-Stanisic

Library of Congress Cataloging-in-Publication Data has been applied for.

ISBN 978-0-06-287934-9

19 20 21 22 23   LSC   10 9 8 7 6 5 4 3 2 1

This book is for my mother, and the rest of my equally beautiful, funny, outspoken family
—B., B., W., G.

No advanced step taken by women has been so bitterly contested as that of speaking in public. For nothing which they have attempted, not even to secure the suffrage, have they been so abused, condemned and antagonized.

—Susan B. Anthony, *Fifty Years of Work for Woman*
(February 15, 1900)

Contents

x   Contents

Introduction

I was a teenager when I first watched Disney's version of *The Little Mermaid*. Two hours later I was as much a fool for Ariel as anybody else. I knew the Hans Christian Andersen story it was based upon, having come across it as a little girl—before I knew enough of the world to be bothered by the fact that Andersen's mermaid suffered stabs like steak knives when she walked on land and that when she wasn't singing with her remarkably lovely voice, she was notably silent. Disney's Ariel was so much more appealing. She cavorted with dolphins, rumbled with sharks, and had a calypso-singing crab as a sidekick. Apart from all that, we had something in common: we both loved to use our voices.

I'd long since memorized each one of Ariel's songs by the time I became a mother and had matured enough to abandon my teenage obsession with Ariel's perfect, bouncy red bangs. It hadn't occurred to my younger self that my hair never looked as good as Ariel's, because she was a cartoon character.

It wasn't until I watched the movie with my son that I realized what was troubling me. It was subtle at first. When Ariel surrendered her voice in its entirety to the Sea Witch, I felt the first stirrings. Swapping her voice in exchange for human legs on a fool's quest to win Prince Eric seemed like a patently bad idea. After all, her voice was most of what he knew of her. It was her lovely singing voice the prince first heard as Ariel rescued him from that shipwreck. Without it, how could she convey to him all the things that she was? The daughter of a sea king, a collector, a defier of sharks?

Even Andersen's original little mermaid had a moment of doubt. "But if you take away my voice, what is left for me?" she asks the Sea Witch. It was the right question to ask and remains so today.

"You'll have your looks," Disney's Sea Witch assures Ariel. "Your pretty face. And don't underestimate the importance of body language."

In other words, what girl needs a voice when she has a body? Of course, the Sea Witch may have known all along that Ariel's sense of self was wrapped up in her voice. Ariel doesn't totally succeed with Prince Eric until she has her voice back, but she comes awfully close to getting that kiss. Her looks, her pretty face, were almost enough to get the job done.

But something more fundamental was bothering me about *The Little Mermaid*: Ariel *chose* to give up her voice.

I've built my career around my voice. After studying to be an opera singer in college, I graduated with a degree in vocal performance and found my way to Wisconsin Public Radio. There I shook hands with my tour guide, the station's velvet-voiced chief announcer, who showed me the music library, the studios, the station's full-size grand piano sprawled enticingly upon dated parquet floors. At the end of our tour, he looked into my eyes and changed my life. "You don't have any speech defects," he said. "Do you want to be on the air?"

I didn't, actually. I was only hoping to find a job where I could get paid to write. But when someone asks you if you want to be on the radio, you say yes. And I'm forever grateful that I did. Eventually I became a senior producer and contributor on the nationally syndicated program *To the Best of Our Knowledge*. The team and I hold a Peabody Award for our work on the show in 2004. Later I hosted my own program, *The Veronica Rueckert Show*; cofounded and cohosted the radio news magazine *Central Time*; and began a public-speaking and story-coaching company built to empower women to learn to use their voices as instruments of strength and personal expression. Over the years on the radio, I had the opportunity to talk with creators, performers, and thinkers who ran the gamut from feminist Gloria Steinem to former secretary of state Madeleine Albright. For all of these conversations—and every other one besides—I have needed a voice.

The human voice is a marvel. In a world with billions of people, your voice is unique. It's shaped by the way your parents spoke, by where you live, by how your body is formed, and by the resonance spaces in your head, neck, and chest. It's shaped by how you feel about yourself. Your voice is a unique fingerprint of who you are and a truer image of the self than almost any other part of your physical being.

I love nothing so well as the sound of the human voice. I have trouble with names, but I imprint voices and carry them with me forever: the lush four-part harmonies of the band Great Big Sea, sung to a crowd in the tiny black-box bar where I first saw them; the bubbling warmth of Anna Pavord enthusing about the flower that drove seventeenth-century Western Europe into a frenzy. She is the reason I fill my house with tulips. My music school classmate Nate Stampley rehearsing Ralph Vaughan Williams's bittersweet *Songs of Travel*—the first time I ever heard them—in an empty concert hall; the bottomless love in the voice of Sister Priya; and the unselfconscious sound of my kids belting out *Hamilton* in the back seat of my car. These are the voices I carry with me. The music of them is stamped on my soul. I love my own voice, too.

Most of the time when I ask the women in my workshops or the audiences at my talks if they love their own voices, the answer is no. A stray person or two might think her voice is a little okay, but most of them flat out don't even *like* it. Here's what's so sad about that: without a positive relationship with such a key part of ourselves, it's challenging to share what's inside—the ideas, the love, the passion, and, most of all, the potential.

The way we feel about ourselves is inextricably linked with our voice. The vocal instrument is housed in the body, so that makes any ambivalence we have about our physical selves part of the relationship we have with our voice.

I worked with one woman who, as a child, had been choked by a neighborhood boy. He had clamped his hands around her neck, and when she had tried to scream for help, she couldn't. To this day, she has nightmares about not being able to speak and has a complicated relationship with her voice. She says that if she can get away with it, she'd rather be silent than talk. To be clear, there's nothing wrong with being an introvert or desiring silence, but she came to me to find a new pathway toward a positive relationship with her voice. Another woman I worked with, an attorney, had just been made partner but didn't feel she had reached her leadership potential. As part of her exploration of how to express herself more fully, she worked with me to strengthen her voice, take a stronger stance at meetings, and bring the full dynamic range of her voice into play when she spoke. For her, the voice was a conduit for self-expression and leadership.

The voice is an amazing gift, both a privilege and a responsibility. Using it takes courage, especially if you're a woman. We're given only a finite amount of time to figure out what it's for, to grow into ourselves enough that we can speak up when the time comes.

Yet a woman's right to speak in public is a right that hasn't been fully granted. Modern research backs this up. In a study of deliberative groups designed to mirror Congress in their gender makeup, women used only 60 percent of the floor time used by the average man. Women are interrupted more often than men, both by men and by other women. Women of color may be disrespected at even greater rates when they speak. A revealing study of the US Supreme Court found that women justices were three times as likely to be interrupted as their male colleagues. Things were even worse for the only woman of color on the court.

In 2012, a Yale University study found that when hypothetical women executives talked more often than their peers, study respondents rated their competency down by 14 percent. But when male executives did the same, their competency rating went *up* by 10 percent.

This is the tightrope women walk. If we speak too much, we're seen as pushy or aggressive; we face a backlash. If we don't speak at all, we're relegated to the sidelines and run the risk of being perceived as passive and ineffectual.

Young women in particular have it tough. Though Generation X had, like, Valley Girl Speak, millennial women have vocal fry. The gravelly tone is reminiscent, apparently, of bacon sputtering in a pan, and women—especially young women— are being criticized for having it and are facing real consequences. More than once, people have confided in me that they subtract IQ points when they hear it—even though they may not want to—and women with vocal fry may be less likely to land jobs or key assignments at work.

Young women are already being told that they need a thigh gap, perfect grades, and Instagram pics that make them look effortlessly hot—and now they can't even talk the way they want to? Culturally, vocal fry has gone from a pet peeve to a feminist issue, where it remains, at the moment, unresolved. Though vocal fry can on occasion cause real harm to the voice, it's a style that everyone dips into now and again, men and women alike. To fry or not to fry should always be a personal choice. For now, the controversy is one more cultural force compelling women not to talk.

One study of New York State found that male attorneys are far more likely to do the talking than women—with women acting as lead attorneys only 25 percent of the time in the state's private sector and criminal cases, and at low rates across the board. In a world where more than half of all law school graduates are women, the study suggests that male attorneys will do most of the talking, while female lawyers confer in whispers.

Women's voices get the back seat even in the fictional worlds we weave from whole cloth. In Hollywood, women spoke less than a third of the time in the top nine hundred films between 2007 and 2016. And they were far more likely to be partially nude than men were. Undressed and mute: not exactly a nourishing vision for the next generation.

Imagine a world in which women speak half the time in politics. Half the time in board meetings. Half the lines in movies. Half the time on TV, on the radio, in the courtroom, at the

United Nations. And when women do speak, they are taken seriously, judged not by the superficialities of their voices but by the content of their ideas. Where girls are used to hearing the sound of women's voices in places of power and are raised knowing the value of their own voices.

Culturally, we are working to close the wage and leadership gaps for women. Alongside that, we need to close the speaking gap. It's been a long time since women fought for the right to speak in public, but the data clearly show that those days aren't behind us yet.

As a woman in radio, when I was occasionally daunted by the prospect of interviews with politicians or actors or thought leaders, I leaned on the simple act of speaking, one human being to another, to find my way through, reminding myself that I had the right and the obligation to ask questions to reach a deeper understanding. I learned what it is to connect deeply with another human being with nothing more in common than a high-quality phone line. I learned how and when to interrupt.

In today's world, where even magical mermaids must give up their chance to speak to get by, using your voice will change your life. It will give you a mechanism to influence situations directly; it will sharpen the shape of your desires and your beliefs about whether you're capable enough to fulfill them. At work, your voice will be a springboard for your ideas and a whetstone for your sense of agency. In your personal relationships, the addition of your full-throated voice will assert your needs and help you find your way to the person you really are. The world around you will change, too. When you use your voice, you take up your rightful place as a full citizen of the city, state, country, and planet you come from. Learning to use my voice has been among the most cherished gifts of my lifetime. Now the time is here for you to use yours.

OUTSPOKEN

OUTSPOKEN

OUTSPOKEN

OUTSPOKEN

OUTSPOKEN

OUTSPOKEN

OUTSPOKEN

OUTSPOKEN

OUTSPOKEN

CHAPTER 1

Learning to Inhale

On a very special day, you were born. A doctor or midwife helped to clear your nose and mouth of mucus, and eventually you yielded to the sudden imperative to expand your lungs with oxygen and expel carbon dioxide. For the first time ever, you used that air to find your voice. And then you cried.

As miraculous as that first, primal yawp after birth may be, most women are pressured into toning it down, smoothing out the edges, and, in general, learning the unfortunate, life-long lesson of taking up less space and doing so quietly. Along the way, we are aided and abetted in the process of becoming small by a culture that rewards us in the short term for doing so. As we grow up, we are taught to cross our legs, suck in our bellies, keep our elbows tucked in to our sides, and strive to be what used to be called ladylike. The concept survives today under the umbrella of words such as *contained*, *mysterious*, and *demure*. Entire industries exist to help.

YOUR BODY ON LOCKDOWN

You're probably familiar with Spanx, the legendary fabric springy enough to slingshot a pint of Häagen-Dazs to the moon, which was invented when its enterprising founder, Sara Blakely, wanted her butt to look better in a pair of white pants. Blakely took a pair of scissors and snipped off the bottoms of a pair of pantyhose, leaving just the tummy and thigh control portions in place, and voilà! Spanx was born. Blakely became a billionaire on the strength of her business acumen, word-of-mouth marketing, and celebrity endorsements, which led to droves of A-list actresses wearing her garments beneath million-dollar gowns on the red carpet.

Spanx is the latest in a long line of devices manufactured to help us enact a desire as old as time: to mold our bodies into shapes unheard of in nature. But there's a catch, and it's a big one: when we tamp down the process of healthy breath production, we also make it harder to project ourselves into the world. There is a direct relationship between the way we, as women, distort our bodies to appear small and the difficulty we have asserting our ideas, desires, and worth, particularly in male-dominated spheres of power and influence. By understanding this relationship and learning to harness it, women—individually and together—can make significant strides in freeing our voices and expressing ourselves.

Body consciousness for women begins at a young age. One study of body dissatisfaction among young children found that more than half of girls between ages six and eight indicate that their ideal body is thinner than the one they have. And by the time they're seven years old, one in four children has dabbled in some kind of dieting behavior.

The societal pressure for women and girls to take up less space runs deep. Stomach in, legs crossed is a default position for a lot of us, whether or not we're on the subway or sitting next to the Queen of England. In principle, there's nothing inherently wrong with wanting to look your best, which for some of us means a pouf-free stomach and a springy derrière. Body size can (but does not always) correlate with good health, but the body we desire often goes far beyond that.

Harriet Brown, an advocate of the Health at Every Size movement and the author of *Body of Truth*, says that ultimately the science on weight loss shows that efforts to slim down long term are almost always doomed, and that evidence suggests we'd do well to discard our assumptions about the correlation between weight and good health. Among numerous studies, she cites research from the Centers for Disease Control and Prevention that found that mortality rates were the highest for people whose BMI was either very high—or very low.

Women feel it, along with children at younger and younger ages—the imperative to look like the airbrushed bodies in

magazines or ninety-six-pound ballerinas with sunken collar-
bones and the waists of prizewinning greyhounds. Since,
statistically, very few of us do look like that however many
hours we spend at the gym, we're willing to resort to other
means.

Our association with tricked-out underwear goes back
hundreds of years. In the 1700s to 1800s, corsets were the
fashion of the day, and women—including Margaret Mitchell's
femme fatale Scarlett O'Hara—vied for tiny waists. O'Hara's
was the smallest in three counties in *Gone with the Wind*, a
signifier that she was a cut above the rest. Women in corsets
were known to faint or even to suffer internal organ damage
due to the immense inward pressure. The garments were
typically constructed of whalebone, which was not bone at
all but flexible material taken from the jaws of baleen whales,
and later on steel, which was cinched up the back, often with
crisscrossing laces.

In book seven of Laura Ingalls Wilder's Little House on the
Prairie series, Laura and her sister Carrie talk about wearing
corsets. The eldest sister, Mary, wears corsets regularly; Laura
wears them—but resentfully; and Carrie, the youngest, is still
enjoying life without them. Relief was hard to come by for
Laura, and she clung to the little corset-free time she had.
"'You should wear them at night,' Ma said. Mary did, but
Laura could not bear at night the torment of the steels that
would not let her draw a deep breath."

Newspapers from the heyday of the corset report mothers
and daughters tussling about whether or not to loosen or

remove corsets at night, as Laura did. At least a few mothers tied their daughters' hands to keep them from sneaking some corset-free relief. But it wasn't just mothers who worried that their daughters might develop a so-called clumsy figure; employers had a say in the matter, too. In the *Evening Post*, a shopgirl shared her story in 1899:

> *It is only two months ago that my employer insisted upon my reducing my waist from 16in to 14in, on the ground that she must have a model to show the newest fashions on. How could I refuse? I know many girls who would lace their waists till they fainted to get a good situation. And so to please these ladies I am locked day and night into a vice which hardly allows me to breathe.*

From corsets and girdles to the contour wear of today, molding our bodies into unusual shapes is a habit that is closely intertwined with our willingness to sacrifice something infinitely precious and powerful: the ability to breathe deeply.

On Instagram, the Kardashian family is a key part of the body-shaping revival, plugging so-called waist trainers—a lower-sitting version of the corset that is notoriously difficult to wriggle into. Khloé Kardashian posted pictures of herself online in her waist trainer, and the size of her middle raised calls of alarm and disapproval from some of her followers, which may be evidence that at least some things have changed. Then again, the internet is loaded with the stories of other women who rushed out to try waist trainers themselves.

Nonetheless, Laura Ingalls Wilder would have recognized some of the same concerns about corsets being raised by today's aggressive shapewear that date back hundreds of years, with or without the scientific language to describe them. In *Elle* magazine, the gastroenterologist Dr. Roshini Rajapaksa weighed in on the phenomenon, saying that garments that "push your stomach contents up towards your esophagus" theoretically increase the risk of acid reflux. Other possible, more severe maladies include displaced organs, compressed lungs, or fractured ribs. Many women have been convinced to pay the price.

We can rearrange our anatomy only to a certain degree. We can push and compress and hoist until at last we hit the limit: maybe we can't Houdini out of our bodysuit fast enough in the bathroom. Or a viciously suppressed area of flesh looking for an escape route makes itself known with an urgent pop, like a game of whack-a-mole. Or something far worse happens: we can't breathe. And when we can't breathe, it's time to call it quits. Because nothing is worth that. If we don't jealously guard our voices and remember to use them, we can lose the thread of something indescribably dear.

CONFIDENCE COLLAPSE

When we hit the speed bumps of life, our relationship with our breath can be a lifeline back to ourselves. There's a reason we feel like someone sucker punched us in the gut when we lose confidence. Whether we know it or not, the attention we pay to our breath is inextricably linked to the respect we pay ourselves. My voice teacher used to tell me, "Breathe to the place you feel the pain." At the time I thought it was shoddily conceived hocus-pocus, but after more than a decade of wondering what on earth she meant, I realized that when we have emotional pain or a collapse of confidence, we tend to seize up in the region of the body we most closely associate with the negative emotion, such as fear or shame or pain— we'll hold it in suspension like a cherry trapped unnaturally in a 1950s Jell-O salad. The full, easy movement of breath can help release the pain or fear and allow energy to move freely through the body again. It sounds like a metaphor, but it's not. Think of what happens when you are afraid. Do you forget to breathe? When you're very sad, do you curl into a ball? When our confidence deserts us, our breath—and a renewal of our voice—can bring it back.

There was a time in my life when I stopped trusting my voice. My blue period arrived during the in-between years: after college graduation, before meaningful work. I felt inconsequential and thirsty for something I couldn't name. I had majored in voice, but I wasn't sure I wanted to go any further down that road. My friends had dispersed with the winds—to Paris, to New York, to Chicago—and I stayed behind, growing more silent and more strained. I didn't remember how to believe in myself, how to live easily in my own skin. I put my music away and stopped singing.

Something had to change. Each night before bed, I'd take out a few old pictures of myself from childhood—and I'd see her: a little girl with her arms stretched wide, a huge smile, and bright eyes without a cloud of doubt, a child at home in the world who knew without anyone telling her that she had a right to be. I would try to imagine myself back into the mind of that girl, as if seeing could make me whole again. At the time, everything had gone gray. I couldn't even call up the memory of everyday raptures—thunder during a spring storm, the sweet ache in my stomach from long and lasting laughter. But somehow looking back across the years and working my way from the outside in brought me back to myself. In those photos, self-confidence hadn't been something I worked at; it had been simply me. Projecting my voice into the world then hadn't been a matter of force, because my natural language was song, and from that spirit—that cherishing of the sound of me—my voice had had a platform to grow.

Growing up the child of a young, single mother, I was always enveloped in love. It hadn't worked out between my parents, so my mother and I were complete unto ourselves. We were Lorelai and Rory without the rich grandparents or the good metabolisms, but we had love and we were happy. We were also poor. In the pictures, I'm wearing things like saddle shoes and bell-bottoms of questionable provenance and taste. Even while working and getting her master's degree, my mother took care of me herself, save for visits to my grandparents, a two-hour car ride away. Sometimes I had hideous, home-styled haircuts that looked as though they'd been executed using a medieval wheat-thatching device. Other times my hair looked better and I was captured clutching a pet—maybe a doomed but hard-loved brown hamster. It didn't matter if I looked like a refugee from the Black Death or a sleek child of the early 1980s. Either way, I was unselfconscious and very, very happy. Not in one shot were my arms crossed in shame over my belly or my shoulders hunched protectively toward my ears.

I had been a happy child. "We used to bike all over Madison," my mother remembered. "You rode in that baby seat on the back, and you would sing the entire time. I couldn't get you to stop, even when I stopped to talk to someone." And she was right—I remembered it, too.

I had grown up in a matriarchal household where women's voices were the only voices. My mom to this day is a feminist with a booming voice and a strong point of view. She taught me to be unselfconscious about using my voice and drove the lesson home by taking me on nighttime trips through the state parks of Wisconsin. With my godmother, we'd hang out the windows of the car and hoot into the dark forest, doing our best to call down barred owls during their mating season, in March, when the ice on Cox Hollow Lake was thin and crackly. We sounded stupid and loud—infinitely unladylike and undignified—but we didn't care. It was too much fun hooting up into the night sky. Enchanted despite their better judgment, the owls flew closer and answered. It was the best kind of night music.

The memory of how I had gloried in my voice, how at

home I had felt in my body, jogged something lost into place in those blue-shaded days. I began to play the piano and sing. It was spring, and my voice carried out the open windows over the sidewalks and down to the street. Sometimes dogs howled along or neighbors stopped to listen, and I found I didn't mind. It wasn't a barred owl's call, but I was back.

TAKE UP SPACE

In 2014, the Metropolitan Transit Authority in New York City instituted a new ad campaign. One of its posters read, "Dude . . . Stop the Spread, Please." The posters were targeting a phenomenon that had finally earned a name: manspreading. The term referred to men in public places who sit with their legs spread out in a kind of V shape, often taking up two or three seats instead of one. *The Oxford English Dictionary* added it to the lexicon in 2015.

Just before the MTA launched its new effort, the *New York Times* covered the manspreading campaign and quoted twenty-year-old Fabio Panceiro, who said, "I'm not going to cross my legs like ladies do. I'm going to sit how I want to sit."

Like almost anything related to gender, the manspreading campaign evoked a backlash. Online, a movement sprang up charging women with "she-bagging," or hogging extra seats with bags instead of bodies. Even the occasional feminist accused the movement of being shallow or trivial. But the city of Madrid disagreed. In June 2017, it banned manspreading from all public transport with new signage depicting unacceptable behavior by riders. In Madrid's case, the signs showed a cartoon person with legs spread wide onto the seats next to (presumably) him with a scoldy X in the upper-left-hand corner.

Issues of common decency aside, science has found some compelling reasons for women to join men in living large. A pair of studies from UC Berkeley give the question of spreading out some revealing data points. In the first, behavioral scientist Tanya Vacharkulksemsuk and her team watched 144 videos of speed-dating participants, then correlated the videos with ratings doled out by the other speed daters. The finding? Both men and women who used more open body language were seen as more attractive. The "manspreading" participants doubled their chance of getting a second date.

In the second study, she posted pictures of women and men in expansive body postures on a dating site. In response, 87 percent of men were picked in response to their open body stances, while 53 percent of women got the nod for the same expansiveness. The bigger (aka manspreading) postures of both women and men were also perceived as more dominant. In an overarching sense, this correlation of an open body posture with dominance is key for women.

Apparently, it's not just men who are more appealing when they hold their bodies in bigger, bolder ways. Even so, it's almost impossible to find pictures of women in expansive postures—the exception, of course, being the photos of women in "power poses" that cropped up in the wake of Amy Cuddy's 2012 viral TED talk, "Your Body Language May Shape Who

You Are," and best-selling book, *Presence: Bringing Your Boldest Self to Your Biggest Challenges.* The psychologist's findings seemed to show that when women assumed "superhero" postures for a given amount of time, their testosterone levels and tolerance for risk went up. Around the country, women copped Superwoman stances before they hit the boardroom. But Cuddy's theory came into question when new experiments failed to replicate the results.

However, beyond research that suggests that open body postures are seen as more dominant (as well as more attractive), there's a more profound reason for spreading out: you can breathe.

BE HEARD

To allow yourself the extravagance of a full, grounding breath can feel strangely risky, as though you are somehow taking too much. More than you deserve. But it's exactly what you deserve, and it is the best kind of risk. It will change your sense of self, and it will change your voice. You may come face-to-face with your inner Beyoncé, the woman inside you who embraces the strength of her voice and isn't about to sit quietly in the corner. Be warned: you may draw reactions you didn't expect when you are too strong or too free or too . . . audible.

When I was in grade school, I had the loudest voice in the summer musical. I loved to sing and belted out songs at the top of my lungs. But one day during rehearsal, the director halted the song and singled me out. She said, "Veronica, I need you to sing a little softer. We can't hear anyone but you."

For a shy kid like I was then, it was a tough moment. I remember the dusty smell of the gym we were practicing in and the feeling of wanting to sink deep inside myself and find a place to hide.

For me, singing wasn't just a pastime; it was part of who I was. So, I kept doing it. But I became more tentative and began the yearslong work of siphoning away some of my power so it didn't show. After a while, it became routine, and I stopped remembering what it was like to sing at full tilt. I held myself in permanent check.

That feeling of caution carried over to the way I conducted myself in my day-to-day life. If singing too loudly was un-desirable, surely talking too loudly was problematic as well, as was being the loudest voice in the room. Women are often excellent team players. It's possible that we can put at least part of this down to values of inclusion and open communication, but perhaps part of it is that we're taught not to stand out too much as individuals but rather to blend in for the good of the group. To assimilate like the hive-minded Borg on *Star Trek*.

One day years later in college, my voice professor was looking for more from me in a song by Enrique Granados, a Spanish composer I loved to sing. In an exercise I do to-day with my clients, we faced off against each other, palm to palm, with one foot braced behind us, and as I sang, she pushed me with all her might. She was in her early seventies but nearly six feet tall and a towering force when roused. That day she was wearing her Desert Storm sweatshirt, an ominous signal to the students that meant buckle up, buttercup, it's about to get real.

My arms and legs trembled with the effort of keeping myself from toppling backward against her relentless pressure as I sang. And then, from somewhere inside me, came a powerful, full-throated, uninhibited sound I hadn't heard since that day years ago in a dusty school gym. My professor released her hands and stood back, looked me in the eye, and said, "Well. Now where did that come from?"

We don't teach women to be loud in our society. And when they are, we find ways to quiet them, even when we don't mean to, even when we consider ourselves fair-minded, and even when we're consciously trying to do the opposite. To change this will require understanding and conscious, brick-by-brick building toward a different kind of world for the voices of women and girls. Now, decades after that breakthrough in my voice professor's studio, I remember the moment and continue the daily hard work of clearing the way for my voice. Even today, it's not automatic for me. But that's okay. Persistent change requires attention, and once we grant that gift to ourselves, we will never turn back.

Many women have a story like mine, a story that began the uneasy relationship they have with their voice and their ability to share it later in life. Once you recognize the issue, you can begin the process of learning to unfurl yourself.

At my talks, I get at this same idea by sharing the story of manspreading. Invariably at least one or two people already know what it is. Sometimes I show a picture of a guy on the subway looking really pleased while he takes up three seats. And then a picture of what I call "the Lady Pretzel"—the default for most of us, sitting with legs crossed and arms folded. Next, I ask my audience to try it themselves with a partner. One of them spreads out with arms and legs, getting into her partner's space by leaning forward, or lounges back like Jeff Bridges swigging a White Russian in *The Big Lebowski*. They talk together for a little while, and then they switch it up and the Manspreader becomes the Lady Pretzel.

Sometimes all this takes a little coaxing, because to many of us, it doesn't come naturally to take up that much space. It feels weird. There's a lot of laughing, some of it self-conscious. It's a delight to give women the permission to let their bodies take up as much room as they can handle. Once in a while, there are guys in the audience. But gender doesn't end up mattering that much—everyone says the same few things about the exercise. In the manspreading posture, they feel empowered to talk longer and louder. They feel in control, and they run the conversation. In the Lady Pretzel position, they feel more subservient, and their voices are softer. Some participants, the really honest ones, report feeling pissed off at the Manspreader in their space.

As a final exercise, I ask everybody to get into the Lady Pretzel position and attempt a deep, full, low breath. They can't do it, at least not well. Their bodies are too closed off and folded up to release the abdomen. A tight leg cross almost always chops off the breath around the belly button. But once they switch into a more expansive posture, they can breathe again. If you can't take a deep, sustaining breath in yoga pants on a Saturday morning, how can you possibly do it in iron underwear in front of two hundred people? Or, God forbid, on national television?

I make no claims about increased testosterone or attractiveness or even dominance, but one thing I know for sure—you cannot feel at the top of your game if you can't breathe. And you certainly won't own the room.

I looked long and hard for photos of women (who weren't in one of Amy Cuddy's "power poses") in expansive body postures. I surveyed the shots from women's leadership events. I looked at thought leaders, politicians, and performers, trying to find someone who didn't default to a variation of the Lady Pretzel, or even better, a role model who looked at home taking up space or passed the "air in the armpits" test for confident upper-body posture. I came up with only a sparse handful: German chancellor Angela Merkel is party on the top, pretzel on the bottom, as is former secretary of state Madeleine Albright. Beyond them, top honors go to Republican senator Susan Collins from Maine, the actress Carrie Coon—who is fearless and completely at ease in her body postures—the feminist icon Gloria Steinem, and naturally Oprah.

One woman who attended a workshop I taught took it all the way. Her work life included regular meetings with difficult and domineering personalities. In response, she told me, she leans all the way back in her chair and puts her feet on the conference room table when she needs to exert her presence. Not everybody has that variety of chutzpah, nor the capacity for risk-taking. But for men and women alike, returning to baseline—feet flat on the floor, knees slightly apart, shoulders back, lower abdomen released—is postural ground zero. It makes room for the breath and lets the body do its job.

WHEN THE OUTSIDE REFLECTS THE INSIDE

Collapsed body posture can be a sign of collapsed internal confidence. Learning to recognize the warning signals of internal confidence collapse is a key tool to holding ground for women. This kind of collapse can happen for a lot of reasons: internal self-talk, external circumstances, and as the body's natural response to stress. Your heart may start to beat more quickly, your breath become shallow, and your thoughts harder to lasso onto cohesive tracks. It can also thrust you into the danger zone for fight-or-flight mode. Thankfully, monitoring yourself closely is an easy, potent tool for successful self-management. In some cases, focusing too much on the reactions of the people around you can be counterproductive if you're working a tough room. Noting every vacant gaze or furrowed brow can translate into negative self-talk: *Why does my boss look bored? My client looks angry—is it something I said?*

It can take only a moment or two to spiral downward into dismal thought patterns that have the potential to derail you.

When you feel the first tendrils of that kind of internal confidence collapse coming, it's time to zip back to your baseline as quickly as you can and work with your body. Do this even before you correct your thoughts. It's that important.

Physically, a collapse can be subtle. Maybe your shoulders round and your spine slouches. You might find yourself balling up your fists and clenching your stomach. Or one of the biggest tells of all—holding your breath. Let's call this hedgehog mode.

When you catch your body collapsing into hedgehog mode in any situation, it's time to consciously release your stomach and begin taking deep belly breaths. Then pull your shoulders back and straighten your spine. That's step one. Now that you've unclenched your body and breath, you're out of defense mode. To pull the wheel in the other direction, to gather your power and assert it, it's time to take up more space. Sitting or standing, widen the space between your knees. Throw an arm around the chair next to you or begin to talk with your hands or arms in broad gestures—make sure you use your full arm, as gluing the elbows to the sides of your body and moving only your forearms tends to undercut the strength of the gesture and makes you look like a bit like an insecure Tyrannosaurus rex.

Warning: this will feel foreign. Your lifelong conditioning will scream at you to return to hedgehog mode at once and stop being so ridiculously and needlessly vulnerable. Uncurling yourself by expanding your chest and straightening your shoulders will make you feel exposed, but see it for what it is:

strength. And remember, open body posture is not, in fact, making you look like a rampaging silverback gorilla—it's simply projecting confidence. Stay the course. Remember, women aren't used to taking up space, which means those first steps toward a larger physical footprint are likely to feel strange and unsettling. At first you'll think you're in the red zone, overshooting the mark and moving the needle a full ninety degrees, when in fact you're usually just beginning to budge it. We're terrible judges of ourselves.

Your belly breaths will support your voice and help it stay strong. Resist the urge to talk sotto voce, or half voice. If it takes a while to restore your voice to its fullest dimensions, that's okay, too. This is a journey. Nota bene: if you work in an open-space office, you will need to work extra hard to speak at full voice. The "whisper and wince" experience of open office spaces hits women especially hard, and if they're not careful, they can end up with a speaking voice more like a stage whisper that stays with them even when they're off the clock. (More on that later.)

It can help to buddy up with a friend who can give you feedback. After the big meeting, when you ask your friend if you looked like an irate silverback gorilla, she will say something like "No—in fact, I didn't notice any difference." Or if you're getting good, she'll say you killed it in there and you looked strong and confident.

Remember, as you move into more expansive postures, you can't gauge the success of this exercise by the response at the table. As women respond to the pressure to be silent and small by taking up more space with their voices and bodies, there may be surprise, hostility, and a social pushback. Remind yourself that it is your right to breathe and talk and take up space. It is your right to share your voice and ideas and insights—even if they are not polished and perfect and vetted by committee. Remind yourself that it is time and that you are doing this for yourself and also for your daughters and sons and the generations to come. It is your right to be heard.

THE TALKING GAP

Taking up space isn't just something we do with our bodies.

Not too long ago, on the public radio show I cohosted, we were looking for a reporter to talk about a particular news story. We did our research and found a potential guest who'd been covering the story for weeks. When we asked if she could join us for an interview, she told us she didn't feel prepared or knowledgeable enough to talk for twelve minutes about the subject. We pressed a little, but she demurred. In a pinch, with the deadline looming, we got in touch with her colleague. He hadn't been covering the story at all but told us he'd be happy to read up on it and join us live on the show later that day. So we ended up talking with a man who wasn't an expert when we should have been talking with a woman who was.

There are overlaps here between the idea of giving yourself permission to take up space and the terrain covered in the book *The Confidence Code: The Science and Art of Self-Assurance*—

What Women Should Know by Katty Kay and Claire Shipman. Kay and Shipman outline the ways women undercut themselves, feel like imposters, or generally deem themselves unworthy in comparison to their male colleagues of similar standing. Another way to look at the issue of bridging the confidence gap between men and women is to approach it from the problem of the talking divide: women take up less space with their voices.

Despite the persistent cultural insistence that women talk more than men, we don't—at least not in big group professional settings. Research from Northeastern University took a swing at the "Who talks the most?" question in 2014 and found that women tended to talk more than men in social and collaborative settings (and mostly to each other), while men clearly dominated in professional groups of six or more people.

Perhaps if we all paid a little more attention to the incredible instrument we house right in our own bodies, we'd realize that the voice is one of the greatest gifts we have, and we would remember that it's our privilege and obligation to use it, even when it's tough.

By following a few basic rules of thumb, you can show your voice the love it deserves and begin to attune yourself to its needs, moods, and capacity. When you spend too much time shouting or coughing, your vocal apparatus tenses and your vocal folds slap together until they get red and irritated. Pushing your voice like this can lead to hoarseness, vocal fatigue, or even nodules on the vocal folds. If you struggle with persistent hoarseness, get yourself checked out for acid reflux or other issues by an ENT doctor.

In general, taking care of your voice is less involved than you might expect. You can start by being good to your body. Drink water, and lots of it. Hot water with honey and lemon is a favorite tonic for singers—try it before you give a talk or when you're feeling under the weather. Leave the uptight underwear at home, at least on days when you have a lot of speaking to do, but maybe forever. Let your body unfold, give your belly room to move and release. Appreciate yourself a bit more by giving yourself the gift of breath. Experiment with the idea of taking up more space with your voice—it's an instrument, and instruments were made to be played.

And most important, use your voice. Your voice is yourself. Trust it. Trust the power it holds, the potential it has to move minds and hearts, and the right you have to use it. Know that even a single voice has value. Attach yourself like a barnacle and refuse to let go of this truth: Your voice matters. Use it!

Exercise: Make Friends with Your Belly

- Wear comfy clothes. Stand with your spine straight and shoulders rolled back, with your chest lifted and expanded.

- Take up as much space as your body needs.

- Place one hand flat on your stomach with the index finger positioned over your belly button and the fingers spread out over the abdomen.

- Make a "birthday candle" with your other hand, holding the index finger pointed toward the ceiling, a few inches in front of your mouth, like a candle.

- Take a deep breath. Release the lower abdomen to accommodate the new breath, making sure the shoulders don't creep up and the chest doesn't heave.

- With a forceful puff, blow out your imaginary candle. Your abdominal muscles should contract and your belly button draw back toward your spine. It might feel a bit like the feeling you get in your abdomen when you blow up a giant rubber raft in the summertime. Or a water balloon. Zero in on the hand covering your belly to feel the movement.

- Repeat five times, taking as long as you need to draw in a deep, low breath with a released abdomen. Yes, your stomach will stick out when you breathe, just as it should.

- Stomach not going anywhere? Shoulders popping up? Try the exercise again on the floor or in bed in the morning when you first wake up. It's harder for your shoulders to move and, chances are, your belly is contracting and expanding all on its own already, since you were sleeping.

- Advanced: let's add some sound! Add the word "Ha!" to each candle blow, feeling the fullness and power of the breath and sound.

- Use the belly breath whenever you are anxious, fearful, or over-adrenalinized. You can do it in public without the candle.

- Put both hands on your belly and send it some love. You're going to get along great.

CHAPTER 2

The Sound of You

There are a million and one ways to disappear. One of them is to become so small and silent that you yourself will hardly know you exist. As the years slip past, it's entirely possible to look around and realize you've buried your voice in ninety-nine different ways without any memory of having done so. Luckily, it's never too late to make some noise and reconnect with the sound of yourself. But before you do, there's something I'd like to give you. It's a gift that will imbue your voice with power, your mind with steadiness, and your body with resilience. I want you to know how to breathe.

BREATHE IN, BREATHE OUT, REPEAT

A breath is a beautiful thing. Take a moment to appreciate the fact of it happening right now, whether or not you're paying attention. As to what exactly goes on in the body when we breathe, here's how it works.

When we inhale, air enters our lungs, moving from an area of high pressure to an area of low pressure. Oxygen from the air moves from small sacs in the lungs called alveoli into the pulmonary capillaries. In exchange, the capillaries produce carbon dioxide, which moves up the windpipe and into the environment. That last part is called exhalation.

The diaphragm makes it all possible. The diaphragm is an underestimated swath of muscle and membrane separating the upper body, or thoracic area, from the lower, or abdominal, region. When we contract the diaphragm, it moves outward and downward and we inhale. Our rib cage and belly expand. My voice professor used to tell me to think of this movement as a "thunk," to embed the idea of just how deeply we should feel the breath in the lower abdomen. When the diaphragm relaxes, it moves inward and upward again, and we exhale. Think of the parachute games you may have played in gym class when you were a little kid. Each child held a section of round, rayon parachute and flapped it up into the air in unison. When the nylon puffed up like the top of a hot air balloon, it looked like our belly during inhalation. When we brought it down to the ground, it flattened out, the model of exhalation. Fun fact: when the diaphragm spasms, we get a case of the hiccups.

It's a key part of the whole setup to know that breathing is one of the few bodily functions we can consciously regulate. In other words, you can have a say in the process and direct your body when to breathe in and out, how deeply, and for how long. Your body will, of course, do this all by itself even if you do nothing. But why do nothing when you can work with your breath and make it an ally? The breath can be your genie, your secret weapon, your superpower. In a Robert Schumann song I studied years ago, the beloved I sang about was referred to as the "good spirit," the "better self." That's your breath.

My voice professor in college was obsessed with breath. Sometimes in a dreamy half soliloquy, she'd lean into the grand piano from which she conducted lessons and muse about her death.

"I just wonder," she would say, "what that last breath will be like."

She was more drill sergeant than loving mentor, but I'm forever thankful to her for helping me to get in touch with my body again. To sing, to extend a four-bar line with legato— a seamless, flowing style without any breaks between notes— there's only one way to succeed: to breathe by supporting the voice with the muscles of the lower abdomen. That means allowing the abdomen to grow bigger with breath before it helps produce sound. The human abdomen is built to expand and relax with the movement of breath, to move fluidly and deeply, like an elegant bellows. It helps to remember that the abdomen itself begins at the top hinge of the thighs, far lower than we're used to engaging it.

When you're getting ready for a big meeting, get in touch with your breath ahead of time. One simple technique is to put a bag of party balloons in your desk drawer, and just before you speak, spend a few minutes blowing one of them up, then releasing the air. Repeat a few times. Water balloons are especially tough. This should feel quite a bit like doing a big set of crunches or blowing up a plastic beach ball. The exercise gets your abdominal muscles moving and reminds you of what those muscles are intended to do. Be forewarned: the balloons will make loud, rude noises when you release the air, but hey, it happens to the best of us.

In any workshop I teach, I find that one or two women reverse the natural order; they pull their bellies *in* when they inhale and expand them *out* when they exhale after I ask them to breathe with awareness and pay attention to their abdomen. At first it surprised me. It shouldn't have. I grew up marinating in the same cultural stew as everyone else.

To learn to breathe in a way that restores equilibrium and strengthens the voice is to begin to make peace with your body.

THE MECHANICS

After our first, momentous breath, we rarely think anything about the process of breathing unless we're forced to, due either to illness or to the kind of training that goes along with many contemplative practices such as yoga and meditation.

If the breath is mostly forgotten once we get the hang of it as infants, the physiology of the voice remains almost a complete mystery. Here's how it works.

The vocal cords (also called vocal folds) are housed in the voice box, or larynx. The folds, surrounding muscles, and cartilage are covered in a kind of mucus that helps the whole apparatus function smoothly. That's one reason voice therapists feel that drinking lots of water and running a humidifier in winter are so important! Stretching from front to back, the vocal folds vibrate when air pumped upward from the lungs passes through the narrow opening between them. That vibration is the beginning of a sound wave. The sound moves upward through the pharynx—the cavity behind the nose and mouth—where it is enhanced and emerges as . . . your voice! It's that simple and that miraculous.

THE BEAUTY OF A BREATH

The sympathetic and parasympathetic nervous systems are both part of the autonomic nervous system, which is responsible for largely involuntary bodily processes like digestion, pupil dilation, and heartbeat. The two systems balance each other out. One amps you up, the other chills you out.

Think of them as your two aunties. One auntie is wound tight. She works out, she's a big drama queen, and when she gets triggered, everything gets very crazy very quickly. She's your sympathetic nervous system.

The sympathetic nervous system is what kicks you into fight-or-flight mode when it senses acute danger—like a train headed at you when your foot is stuck in the railroad tracks or a pouncing Bengal tiger. Hopefully nothing like this has ever happened to you, but if it did, you'd thank your sympathetic nervous system for giving you an extra burst of energy and a bracing hit of the stress hormones epinephrine (adrenaline) and norepinephrine. In fight-or-flight mode, you start sucking down air like it's going out of style, your blood pressure spikes, and your body releases extra glucose so you have the fuel to run away or perform a feat of derring-do. Much appreciated when you have a sudden pressing need to lift a car!

The parasympathetic nervous system is your chill auntie. She's a massage therapist, is always drinking turmeric tea, and has a house filled with crystals and singing bowls. When the parasympathetic nervous system is working, your blood pressure falls and your heart rate decreases. Digestion proceeds steadily, and your pupils constrict. The parasympathetic nervous system is associated with "feed-or-breed" and "rest-and-digest" states—much more pleasant than fighting for your life. You may have heard of the principal hormones associated with the parasympathetic nervous system—prolactin and the famous oxytocin, otherwise known at the hormone of love. Last, and not to be overlooked, one other perfectly splendid thing happens when the parasympathetic nervous system is dominant: your breathing slows down.

The vagus nerve is a crucial part of the parasympathetic nervous system. It reaches down from the stem of the brain through the body, connecting to the heart, lungs, and vocal cords, and performs integral functions related to mood, heart rate, and breath. If you stimulate your vagus nerve, you also stimulate the parasympathetic nervous system, thus unwinding the clutches of an overzealous sympathetic nervous system that wants to help you survive that tiger attack. To engage the vagus nerve, you can plunge your head into a vat of cold water. Not an ideal boardroom option. Or you can work with your breath.

The vagus nerve and parasympathetic nervous system are activated when we breathe using the lower abdomen—expanding the lower abdomen when we breathe in and drawing the belly button back toward the spine when we breathe out. It's what our belly does automatically when we sleep calmly and deeply.

If we consciously mediate the length and depth of our breathing, we have the power to move our body from stress and anxiety back toward calm and relaxation. Without our conscious input, our breath will thunder on heedlessly, performing the thankless task of keeping us alive. But if instead we yoke our awareness and intent to its ebb and flow, we can learn a lot about how we truly think, feel, and respond to the world around us. And with that knowledge we can use our breath to intervene on our own behalf and choose to be grounded, well supported, and at ease.

In yogic philosophy, the breath is sometimes visualized as the cord that ties body to soul. Devoted yogis spend a lifetime working with the breath and the energy that flows in and out with it. You don't need to be a lifelong yogi to get started. The virtue of breath awareness is that you can do it wherever you are.

But once you roll back your sleeves and dig in, you'll find that working with the breath is like peeling an onion: there's always another layer. For the act of speaking in public, particularly in high-intensity situations, we need more than air moving into and out of the lungs. To be our best, we need to know how to work with the breath on a deeper level.

Here I am—pretty indisputably alive, you might be thinking, *so I must not be so bad at this breathing thing.* It's hard to argue the point, so let's assume you are alive and breathing in and out on your own just fine.

If there were a Bengal tiger stalking you right now, moving into a pouncing stance, getting ready to leap, what would happen next? Well, in all likelihood, once you spotted the tiger, your nerve cells would fire a message of alarm; your brain would release a spurt of chemicals, including cortisol and adrenaline; your blood pressure would go up; and the blood itself would be rerouted from your digestive tract to your muscles. And your breathing would speed up. This is called fight-or-flight mode, and it was first delineated by Harvard physiologist Walter Cannon in 1915.

In our modern world, we are stalked daily by the metaphorical tigers of conflict, deadlines, performance anxiety, financial worries, and more. As stresses mount or a looming fear creeps closer, it gets easier to flip into Bengal tiger mode, with the adrenals in overdrive and the sympathetic nervous system kicking into gear, getting ready to counter an acute physical threat.

The rise of anxiety is one thumping good reason to make sure you know how to use your breath to calm your body and mind. A 2018 poll by the American Psychiatric Association found that 39 percent of Americans were more stressed than they had been the year before. An additional 39 percent said that they were equally as stressed as the year before, and a mere 19 percent reported feeling less tweaked out than they were.

Generationally, millennials are more anxious than Gen Xers or baby boomers, but boomers aren't entirely basking in their golden years—they experienced a 7-percentage-point anxiety bump between 2017 and 2018. People of color are more anxious than Caucasians by 11 percentage points. And, as you may have intuited already, women are more anxious than men. Overall, we're getting even more freaked out: the nation's anxiety index score jumped by 5 percentage points, to 51 percent, between 2017 and 2018.

Public speaking consistently shows up on lists of people's greatest fears, which makes it a common trigger of the fight-or-flight response. It says something about the times in which we live that a Chapman University study from 2017 showed people found things like corrupt government officials and high medical bills scarier than talking in front of other people. Still, the fear is so pervasive that there's even a name for it: glossophobia.

I've worked with women who had been hit by a sneak panic attack when they'd always been confident speakers in the past. This group is often confused about what's happening and imagines that they're experiencing a heart attack. Sometimes they end up in the ER before they figure out what's really going on.

If you've never lived through a panic attack, thank your lucky stars. They are deeply unpleasant, and the prospect that you could have another one is nearly as bad as the panic attack itself. Then again, the panic attack itself is so wretched, it's hard to top. Symptoms of panic attacks include intense fear, a feeling of impending doom, a pounding heart, chest pain, dizziness, and feelings of disassociation and unreality. That's an incomplete list, by the way.

Anxiety attacks include most of the same symptoms but not usually the sense that you're going to die or the feelings of disassociation and unreality.

During a panic attack, we take rapid, shallow breaths, which cause a sharp decrease in carbon dioxide in the blood, a sensation that, alas, tricks the brain into more panicked, shallow breathing. As you have already surmised, having a panic attack while speaking in public is the stuff of nightmares.

Count me a member of the sneak attack club. Twice in my life, I've been asked to introduce the public radio behemoth and best-selling author David Sedaris when he visited. Both times I was forewarned not to mention his greatest radio hit, "Santaland Diaries," and also not to hug him. Both events were held on the main stage of the Overture Center for the Arts in Madison, Wisconsin, which seats 2,251 people. The first time was a book festival event, where I shared the podium with the festival's director, who was so undeniably at ease in front of an audience that she gave the strong impression of wearing pajamas.

Beforehand, we milled around backstage, listening to the slow-motion crescendo of the theater filling with people. David and his companion arrived last. I assumed that David was the guy I'd seen on the book jacket photos, not the guy with the complicated beard walking beside him. I made eye contact with David, took a step forward, and opened my mouth to say hello.

"No hugging!" The bearded guy flung himself in front of David in a moving display of self-sacrifice. He was completely prepared to take the hug himself if it came to it. I felt the brief, unexpected urge to wrestle David Sedaris to the ground for a Wisconsin bear hug, but the notion sank quickly to the bottom of my agenda. It was slowly dawning on me that I was nervous. My breathing was shallow and growing more so, and I felt the beginnings of a boa constrictor–like grip around my middle, making it impossible to take a deep breath.

A few minutes later, I was standing in the wings, waiting for my cue to enter. David Sedaris stood beside me. "Wow," I said to him, "I'm really nervous."

The last thing I remember before I walked onstage was his reply: "You're *kidding* me."

As the festival director welcomed the audience, I stood at her elbow waiting for my turn and came to the surprise realization that it felt very much like I was going to die.

Jarringly, I registered that the festival director had just concluded her free-flowing welcome by dictating what seemed to be her personal phone number to an audience of more than two thousand people. I hadn't heard the context. My heart was beating as fast as a sprinting tree shrew, and my lungs had become incapable of processing oxygen.

I was used to public speaking—and singing, for that matter. At that time, I hosted radio talk shows for a statewide audience and had recently interviewed former secretary of state Madeleine Albright. I knew the butterflies in my stomach would settle down once I hit my groove.

But this time was different. The director moved aside, and I stepped up to the podium. I was floating above myself, like Shirley MacLaine on one of her out-of-body forays. It was deeply unpleasant.

"I didn't realize we had to give out our phone number," I managed.

The audience laughed. After that I said some words and tried to stay alive. I had to gasp for the little air I had, and every sentence felt impossible. Half my mind was hyperaware that I was talking; the other half thought it would be an extremely good idea to run screaming offstage. The attention of the audience bore down on me like a searing white heat. I finished up, sucking in air as I went—God knows what I said—and slow-motion walked offstage, stopping to shake hands with Sedaris, who looked both completely comfortable and moderately annoyed. It was entirely possible that I'd talked exclusively about "Santaland Diaries" for an entire three minutes.

Afterward I struggled to come to terms with what had happened. It took me a long time to realize that I'd had an anxiety attack. After weeks of digging around online and reading voraciously about causes and cures, I finally figured it out. The knowledge forced me back to square one. I relearned the basics and swore I would never step onstage again without actively working with my breath. Now, before I speak anywhere, I'm prepared. I know what my triggers are. I learn about the venue, what to wear to give myself room to breathe, and what type of microphone will best allow to me to move and channel energy.

It should give us comfort to know we're not alone in this. Not only do the women I coach encounter the same thing, but in the months after my Sedaris fright, I did an interview with a performer who suffered such debilitating panic attacks that he began to explain the condition to his audience and threw buckets of ice water over himself *while performing* when he began to feel anxious. Again, submerging your head in cold water is another way to stimulate the vagus nerve and calm your nerves, but it comes with some obvious drawbacks.

A few years later, I introduced David Sedaris again. Same venue, still no hugs. This time I prepared to the teeth: I memorized the key points of my introduction instead of writing them down, I brought a friend for encouragement, I visualized the event every night beforehand, and I came ready to breathe. And in front of 2,251 people—or thereabouts—I actually enjoyed myself. One day, David Sedaris will finally surrender that single, warm hug and I will be whole.

It's possible to dig ourselves out of a stage-fright hole. But without a working knowledge of how to work with the breath, it's much, much harder.

Five Tips to Overcome Stage Fright

1. **Visit the venue ahead of time.** When you visit, find out where you'll be standing and what kind of podium you'll have or exactly where you'll be seated. Don't be afraid to ask for changes that will make you more comfortable, from a different chair to a larger podium. Request the kind of microphone that suits you best. A lavalier mic will allow you to move around freely, if you'll be standing. A podium with a stationary mic will give you something to grip as you speak and can help you feel grounded.

2. **Move around.** Many speakers with anxiety feel like a butterfly pinned to a specimen board when they speak. Moving around helps dissipate nervous energy that builds up and gives it a healthy channel to flow from you to your audience. You don't need to stalk the stage like a panther, but even taking a few steps and making a few arm gestures can help release anxiety.

3. **Visualize your talk.** If at all possible, memorize your talk in the weeks or days leading up to the event. Then pick a time when you're quiet and feeling relaxed—before going to bed is a good choice—and rehearse your speech mentally. Go over it several times, imagining the audience beaming approval at you while you radiate confidence.

4. **Pick a friendly face in the audience to focus on.** You've heard this advice a million times, but it really does work. Choose someone with an engaged, happy face in the first moments

after you take your place onstage. Either arrange for a friend to smile encouragingly when you look at them or find someone with a consistently warm, kind expression. As you deliver your talk, return to that person periodically as a touchstone to steady yourself and maintain your confidence.

5. **Lengthen your exhalations.** When your breathing begins to get away from you and your anxiety ratchets up, it's time to take the reins. Breathe in to a count of four and out to a count of eight. The four and eight aren't important, but the doubled length of exhalation is. Three and six might work, or five and ten. This lengthened exhalation engages your parasympathetic nervous system and reduces anxiety. This practice is ideal before any event that keeps you awake at night.

CHAPTER 3

To Change or Not to Change?

My grandfather was a plumber from Milwaukee. Although he lived to almost ninety-eight years old, his knees gave up the ghost much earlier after decades spent kneeling on concrete floors in the basements of public schools where he worked endlessly on leaky pipes and cranky boilers. He had wanted to be a pastor, he once told me, but his family couldn't afford the training, so he had learned a trade instead. Even so, he went to church every Sunday without fail and inspired articles in the weekly bulletin about the remarkable devotion he showed to his faith and to my grandmother, even after she needed around-the-clock care to help manage her dementia.

He was not fancy or moneyed. Neither was my grandmother. When, later in life, as her disease progressed, my grandma finally lost enough of her inhibition to say the worst word she could think of, that word was "crap." When my grandparents spoke you could hear working-class, north side Milwaukee—the little box houses, the well-maintained Oldsmobiles, and the unlikely Greek Orthodox church built by Frank Lloyd Wright with its dome of cerulean blue. That's what I heard when they spoke, even if I didn't know it until later. "The heck with you" was the ultimate Rueckert dismissal.

My mom was the first in the family to go to college. She earned a BA in anthropology and then a master's in education. Once in a while she still says, "The heck with you." I grew up far away from my father, who lived in Puebla, Mexico, but I sometimes wonder what I might have sounded like if I'd spent summers sitting around the kitchen table with my *abuela*.

While I worked toward my degree in vocal performance at the University of Wisconsin–Madison, I became more and more attuned to voices. I marinated in the rounded vowels and crisp diction of wannabe opera singers, and my peers gave me grief for saying egg-zit instead of ex-it. Or honking out the *a* in *bagel*. We made fun of the *ae* sound, the telltale Ethel Merman-y American vowel you hear in words such as *man* and *bag*.

My speaking voice evolved along with my singing voice. By sliding my thumb along the roof of my mouth beginning at the front teeth, I could feel exactly where the bone ended and the soft palate began, and I learned to arch the space there to mimic the sensation just before a yawn. By raising my soft palate like that when I spoke or sang, my voice picked up overtones that made it more rich and resonant. It was like adding a new floor to a house. My voice professor taught me to read Shakespeare's sonnets and spit out every letter like I was throwing knives. To warm up, we sang an exercise with the words "the tip of the tongue, the teeth, the lips." It reminded us that the hard work of enunciating came from the front of the mouth. It wasn't necessary to chew on the words so much as keep the movement of the tongue and lips efficient and precise. "What's the one thing we have as singers that the orchestra doesn't?" she'd ask. Consonants was the answer. A crisp *t* or *d* at the end of a word could carry to the back of the hall.

As the years passed as a radio host, the me on the outside began to match the me on the inside. When I was at my best, there was almost perfect alignment between the two. What's more, I could take my voice anywhere and it would serve me well. At the hospital, I could pose a train of questions with confidence and be asked if I was a doctor myself. I could be seated next to the biggest philanthropic muscle in the city at the Wisconsin Chamber Orchestra gala and hold my own about schools and the arts. When I was engaged in an interview and doing my job well, my voice wasn't a conscious thought at all but a response to the connection the interviewee and I were forming and the ideas being shared.

The only problem was this: an overly mannered voice can become a trap. There were times I disguised my feelings of insecurity about a topic with a bland, regal voice. Or when I manipulated a sentence with a hint of vocal fry as a stand-in for real emotion, like I'd heard other people in radio do. If I sounded polished enough, I figured, no one would ever sense my discomfort. At those times, my voice felt like a straitjacket, and I struggled to surface my real self again. It may have sounded fine, but it felt terrible.

At the same time, the culture was changing. A polished, well-modulated voice was no longer desirable or authentic. Ira Glass came along with *This American Life* and launched a thousand radio geeks who heard the message loud and clear: be yourself and tell good stories. Both are excellent maxims for life.

But to say "Be yourself" is to oversimplify. I am the product of both my family roots and my classical training. One aspect was nature, the other nurture. One was a choice, the other completely involuntary. I cherish both aspects of the voice I have today, and I gut-check again and again to make sure I'm not sliding into my faux voice and that I flag it when I am. It matters a lot. When I teach workshops or coach, I see firsthand the pain and discomfort that go along with forcing yourself into a voice that doesn't feel fully your own. If your authentic self is a Birkenstock, wearing a Blahnik will hurt.

ON TORCHES, PITCHFORKS, AND VOCAL FRY

There's a bit the comedian Mary Mack does about how she grew up. It goes, "I grew up in northern Wisconsin. I gotta wear a lot of makeup just to look plain." It plays particularly well in L.A.

Mik, as her friends call her, has spent a lifetime being tough—a trait she picked up from her years in Burnett County. She's appeared on *Last Call with Carson Daly*, *Conan*, and *Last Comic Standing*. Mik ran with the same pack of kids from kindergarten through high school. She wasn't worried about being pretty or popular; she was too busy watching PBS—the only channel her family could get—and hacking the heads off dead fish.

Mik didn't know it at the time, but her voice stood out. It was high pitched and, to an out-of-towner, almost incomprehensible. When she travels today, people can't quite place the north woods *o*'s, and they ask her if she's from Ireland. Once a producer in Hollywood wondered if she thought she could pass for a receptionist from San Diego—the job was on the line. But Mik had to tell the truth, because the last time she'd tried to "fix" her *o*'s, her jaw had actually cramped up with the pain of it. She told the producer no.

Sometimes even Mik can't understand what the hell people are saying when she goes back home after a long spell away.

She tried out a line of unvarnished Burnett County on me, and the *o*'s in the sentence "You guys, I want to go out on the boat, too" sounded to my ears like the first line of a song by a Swedish death metal band.

Like music, science, and film, comedy is still very much a male-dominated industry. Early on in her career, Mik was on the roster at a comedy festival in Australia. But one day, out of the blue, the booker called her agent and said, "We can't have Mary this year because we booked another lady who also has a high voice." It turned out to be Mik's friend Maria Bamford, who grew up an hour away from Burnett County in Duluth, Minnesota.

"At the time I was known for having this quirky voice, and they unbooked me because of it," Mik remembers. "And then I thought, well, how many men have the same register of voice? And if you're concerned about us being from the same area, how many men from New York are in this festival who are all tenors? The answer is many, and they didn't unbook those guys."

Mik's story isn't unique. And it isn't over. Female-attributed vocal mannerisms still offend today (to say nothing of the single novelty slot available saved for women), and the list is a long one: vocal fry, sexy baby voice, uptalk, hedging, apologizing, and breathiness. The term *vocal fry* has been around for decades in speech pathology circles but has, in recent years, broken through the surface of popular culture, where it's sparked passionate debate among generations, genders, and even women's advocates.

Womanspeak: A Handy Guide

VOCAL FRY

What is vocal fry? Vocal fry is the term used to describe vocal production that results in what's been described as a creaky, growling, or rattling effect in the lower register. Food metaphors are popular, too. Fry has been compared to the erratic snaps of corn popping or bacon fat sputtering in a pan. Hence, vocal fry.

You know it. The croaky, I'm-too-bored-to-care vocal texture heard at the bottom of the range in many young women in the United States, rich guys in England, and everybody else at one time or another.

The complaint: Vocal fry is making young women sound incompetent, unmotivated, and kinda dumb.

The counterpoint: Other young women hear vocal fry as confident. Everyone uses vocal fry from time to time. Let's get over it and stop finding excuses to dismiss women's voices.

SEXY BABY

Two words that make you feel creepy to say together, but there they are anyway. Sexy baby voice is seen as a high-pitched, affected voice used by grown women that brings to mind both sexual availability and, well, a baby or a young girl. We are deep into feel-gross *Lolita* territory here.

The complaint: No one will take you seriously with sexy baby voice. It infantilizes you and repels other women, who may see it as an affectation to curry favor with men. You are a grown woman, talk like one.

The counterpoint: It is not sexy baby voice. It is *my* voice.

UPTALK

Also known as upspeak. The vocal practice of inflecting upward with your voice at the end of a statement, thus turning the aforementioned statement into a question, e.g., "My name is Elle? I just got into Harvard?" Uptalk also creates a kind of antecedent-consequent vibe in a conversation. The equivalent of "two bits!" after "Shave and a haircut." The upward inflection may leave the listener wondering if you have more to say, which can cause awkward pauses and false starts, like a bad first date. Related: Tacking a question such as "Do you know what I mean?" onto the end of your statement.

The complaint: It makes you sound insecure, ineffectual, and unsure about what you just said. It may result in a follow-up question, such as "Wait, did you get into Harvard or didn't you?"

The counterpoint: Some women report that uptalk clears conversational space for them to finish and hold the floor for longer periods of time. Without it, they feel they are more likely to be interrupted. Other women use it to soften difficult conversations and content that could be perceived as strident. Women also use uptalk to develop rapport with one another by adding informality to the conversation. Uptalk also gives the listener a chance to listen actively, with a "Right?" or an "Mmm-hmm."

HEDGING

What happens when you have an opinion about something but rather than saying it outright you soften the impact with words and phrases like "sort of," "just," "I think," "maybe," "try," and "I feel like." Related: disclaimers ("I could be wrong, but . . . "; "You probably already thought of this . . .").

The complaint: It dilutes the power of your words and telegraphs a lack of conviction. Many people are drawn to strong leaders. Hedging makes it harder for people to see you as one.

The counterpoint: Women speak differently from men, and rather than ram through strong opinions, they prefer to take their audience and its feelings into consideration. Also, many women would rather be right than overconfident. It's called emotional intelligence, and it's an asset, fool.

OVERAPOLOGIZING

The speech habit of apologizing as a knee-jerk placeholder in numerous situations that do not expressly call for an apology. For instance, "I'm sorry, but I think . . ."

The complaint: Frequently apologizing when you've done nothing wrong undermines your appearance of competency and confidence, even if you've done nothing wrong. It can have the effect of making you look blameworthy instead of charmingly self-effacing and frequently comes across as early career insecurity.

The counterpoint: It's seen as one of the several deadly sins of womanspeak; therefore, people hate it unfairly. The world would be a better place if men apologized as often as women do.

CLASH OF THE FEMINIST TITANS

The feminist author and scholar Naomi Wolf got involved in the debate over womanspeak with an article entitled "Young Women, Give Up the Vocal Fry and Reclaim Your Strong Female Voice." In the piece, she made the case that young women's use of mannerisms such as vocal fry, uptalk, and run-on sentences undermines their authority and makes it difficult to take them seriously. To tell the full story, she quotes numerous young women who say they use qualities like fry and breathiness to appear less threatening or difficult—in essence, she says, to appease the patriarchy. But far from being appeased, Wolf quotes studies and shares anecdotes that make it clear just how annoying the mannerisms can be to the patriarchy and lots of other people besides. An unnamed source compares the sounds of young women talking to ducks quacking. A law partner confides that run-on sentences make it hard to know when a woman has finished saying what she wants to say. In conclusion, Wolf acknowledges the power and accomplishments of a new generation of young women but urges them to cast off the vocal mannerisms imposed upon them by a culture eager to seize upon any excuse to trivialize their voices and ideas, and harness the confidence and strength of their voices. It was a strong plea from a leading feminist voice, but the tide had already started to turn on vocal fry and the policing of women's voices.

Three days after Wolf's piece ran, professor Debbie Cameron published a response on the website In These Times entitled

"An Open Letter to Naomi Wolf: Let Women Speak How They Please." Cameron studies language, gender, and sexuality at Worcester College, University of Oxford, and runs a razor-sharp blog about "some of the linguistic dilemmas confronting feminists in the 21st century" at Language, A Feminist Guide. Cameron began:

> *Dear Naomi,*
> *A few years ago, when you were in Oxford finishing your thesis, you came to one of my lectures on language and gender. So I was disappointed when I saw your latest piece in the* Guardian, *exhorting young women to stop using "destructive speech patterns." Evidently I did a poor job of explaining the basics of my subject. Professional pride compels me to give it another try.*

In her rebuttal, Cameron made the case that young women are frequently at the cutting edge of linguistic innovation, which leads people to the wrong conclusion that new speech patterns are predominantly female. "In time," she said, "the guys will catch up." Next Cameron took issue with Wolf's argument that mannerisms like uptalk and vocal fry have a causal relationship to female powerlessness. To this, Cameron said:

> *That's back-to-front logic: it's a bit like saying that if only African Americans would stop speaking African American English the police would be less likely to shoot them. It*

misses the point that negative attitudes to the language of
subordinate groups are just manifestations of a more gen-
eral prejudice against the groups themselves. People may
claim that their judgments are purely about the speech,
but really they're judgments of the speakers.

The back-and-forth between two titans of feminist scholar-
ship is a microcosm of the ongoing battles around vocal fry
and women's voices. In fact, it stands in for the battles women
have with themselves. As the rallying cry against voice shaming
grows, some women are wondering if they want to change
their voices to conform to a certain strand of professional ex-
pectation or stand their vocal ground and wait for the culture
to shift around them.

Kathryn Arndt was one of the first women to serve on the
board of governors of the American Bar Association. Today
she works with law firms on a number of issues, including
the promotion of women to leadership and management
roles.

"They send me young women and say, 'We'd like to pro-
mote her, but can you please fix her voice?'" Arndt told me.
Typically, she sits down with the woman she's working with
and they talk options and career trajectory. Arndt lays the
choices on the table and sometimes asks, "What if I told you
you could make an extra 100K a year?" Once they hear that,
Arndt says, they're usually ready to make the leap—in this
case to a speech therapist who can help them develop new
vocal production techniques to replace the fry.

All this raises the questions: Can vocal fry hurt your career? And your voice? Even if we're not aware of it, our voices have an impact. Whether you decide to align your voice with industry norms or leave it as is, it pays to go into the professional world with your eyes wide open. No matter what your voice sounds like, using it intentionally is a good on-ramp to using it fully as the instrument that it is.

According to a 2014 study in the journal *PLOS One*, researchers at Duke University found that vocal fry could undermine the success of young women in the labor market. A group of seven men and seven women recorded the phrase "Thank you for considering me for this opportunity" in a normal tone and then again with vocal fry. Then researchers invited hundreds of men and women of various ages to listen to the recordings and complete a survey. It turned out that both men and women listeners preferred voices without vocal fry for men and women, but respondents indicated they'd really rather women's voices to be fry-free, by a small preference margin.

Respondents of both genders said they would be less likely to hire the people with vocal fry and deemed them less trustworthy. And by the way, women had stronger negative reactions to vocal fry than did men.

The speech pathologist Emerald Doll works with patients who have vocal fry and want to correct it at UW–Madison's Voice and Swallowing Clinic. "[Vocal fry is] more used in women as a sign of authority," Doll told me. "You sound more masculine and have a more authoritative perception. Now that perception is changing. Now it's frowned upon."

As far as whether fry hurts the voice, Doll said, "Vocal fry can also sometimes be a sign that there's an underlying physiological problem or pathology but doesn't have to mean there is. . . . I really am fairly unjudgmental as long . . . as you can communicate as you want to and you can be perceived the way you want to." So once again, it comes down to a matter of choice, as long as your fry isn't a signal that something worrisome is going on vocally. The questions remain: How do you sound, and does your voice reflect the person that you are?

EXERCISE FOR VOCAL FRY

1. Say "mmm-hmm" with a closed mouth.
2. Try it again, but draw out the *m*'s an extra-long time, as though you couldn't agree more emphatically with what was just said. The "mmm-hmm" should last a good four seconds. Work on focusing on the vibration and tone of the voice as you draw out "mmm-hmm." It should be very difficult for you to employ vocal fry while saying "mmm-hmm" and equally hard to sound breathy.
3. Now say the phrase "It's a beautiful day" while holding the tone of the voice intact, just as you did on "mmm-hmm."
4. Switch back and forth between the two—first "mmm-hmm" and then "It's a beautiful day." Hang on to the core of your tone until the very end of your sentence.

The idea is to bring the healthy core of the voice you use for "mmm-hmm" over to the sentence "It's a beautiful day."

5.   Repeat as necessary! Anytime your voice spreads or moves into vocal fry territory, try taking a nice long "mmm-hmm" break, then go back into speech. This is also a great exercise for a fatigued voice.

THE FUTURE OF WOMEN'S VOICES

Fact: women's voices usually sound different from men's. Since we are conditioned to hear men talking in public places and positions of power, that means the sound of women doing the same will sound strange and off-putting at first. This is the zone we find ourselves in today. Women don't get pats on the back from the universe for speaking out; there are few rewards. Instead, they are subjected to a steady stream of commentary that often suggests—both obliquely and more directly—that they shouldn't be talking at all. Or that women should sound more like men. But as culture shifts and women are represented in equal numbers to men in the public forum, we will inevitably see increasing tolerance and a wider range of voices.

Susan Stamberg was in the vanguard of this shift. Bill Siemering created the NPR flagship program *All Things Considered* in 1971. A year later, Stamberg became the first female host of the program. She says that to her face, people congratulated her on being a "first," and she was roundly cheered. But behind the scenes it was another matter. On Public Radio Exchange's *To the Best of Our Knowledge*, Stamberg said that eleven years after she first made the move to host, Siemering shared what he'd been hearing from station managers behind the scenes. The comments, according to Stamberg, went like this: a woman's voice is not authoritative, she isn't believable, she will not speak with conviction, people will not take her seriously.

Flash forward: Stamberg is one of *ATC*'s longest-tenured and most beloved hosts. The culture shifted around her as she helped drive it from behind the mic in Washington, DC. Most recently, many of the show's hosts have been women: Audie Cornish, Mary Louise Kelly, Ailsa Chang, and Kelly McEvers.

However, even a "first" like Stamberg says she's not on board with mannerisms like uptalk and vocal fry. She goes so far as to coach guests to think of their voices as "a straight line," so that statements end without an unintentional question mark at the end.

Of vocal fry, she says, "I can't stand it. . . . To my ear it's unlovely, it calls attention to itself, it's distracting, it gets in the way of the information the person is trying to say."

Stamberg is both echoing the sentiment of older generations about vocal fry and also making a strong case that voices affect us deeply. Invest in your voice, and you invest in yourself. No one voice will please everyone, so make sure your voice pleases *you*.

WHEN AUTHENTICITY ISN'T AN OPTION

I met "Tina" at a workshop I was leading one early spring day when the thin layers of ice on the sidewalk still crunched underfoot. In the morning, I talked about the price of code switching for women, of being one person at home and another, unrecognizable person at work. Tina listened to me make the case for authenticity that day, then asked, "What if they don't *want* all of me?" Tina is a tenured professor and the director of her department in the field of communications at a well-regarded university. She has a family, and her paycheck each month helps support them and also relatives in this country and others. "I need this job," she said, "and I get paid well." She wouldn't risk it, she told me, by showing more of her authentic self.

For women of color, Tina said, authenticity is tough. "My dad is an immigrant, so I was always aware of the cost he paid for speaking with an accent. From a very early age I was aware of what it meant to speak to different people in different ways to disguise who you were, which my dad was incapable of doing." The costs are high. Tina says the combined stresses of code switching and working as a black woman in a predominantly white university have given her health problems in the form of chronic illness. For her, authenticity isn't an option.

"In the place I'm working now, when we're talking, it's not like I speak ebonics," she says, "but if I talk the way I talk at home, people literally don't understand what I'm saying. So it's difficult to say 'Be authentic.' . . . It's not that easy." She and other people from marginalized groups face real-world struggles in the pursuit of an authentic voice. As workplaces move toward diversity, they need to move toward creating a space that's safe and welcoming for all voices. In the meantime, women like Tina do what they have to: they shape-shift.

Tina isn't alone in her mode of survival. For decades, women at the leading edge of male-dominated spheres stuck with a formula that worked: put your head down, outwork everybody else, and develop a professional persona that projects the least objectionable version of yourself. A self not unlike that of an Edwardian butler: there when you need him, as quiet as a teapot when you don't.

To survive is to play a game of human Tetris; women twist and contort the unique, sharper aspects of themselves that can make them vulnerable to being knocked out of the game. They modulate qualities like passion, anger, and ambition, which can easily be read as their shadow sides: instability, hormonal moodiness, and selfishness. Never mind that passion, ambition, and even anger are all qualities that can be assets in the quest for the C-suite. Their double-sided nature serves as a negative gender marker for women. Strong personalities and qualities that appear "overly gendered" are risky, so women have often gravitated to the middle of the road, where it's safer— to a neutral presentation style; a controlled demeanor; a careful, well-regulated voice. And it's worked to a certain extent; for decades it helped women climb the ranks alongside their male colleagues, even if the top few rungs were missing from their ladder.

For the women I coach, the process is an emotional one, because they're hearing the voice they've always felt was inside them for the first time, or sometimes it's because they realize that their job has forced them into a false version of themselves—as heard in their voice—and the prospect of living a more integrated, authentic life is an option they never knew they had.

The idea of agency lies at the crux of the question of authenticity. The core question is: Do we *choose* to work with the voice in a way that changes the sound of it because we want to or because we feel internalized shame and inadequacy about it? Are we compelled to change our voice when someone in our life criticizes us and tells us our voice is wrong?

In some cases, women go quiet altogether or face a heightened sense that they're walking a tightrope, with an audience eagerly waiting for them to place a foot falsely and tumble to the ground. As an alternative to confronting colleagues about their behavior or simply looking for a new job, some women try to change themselves. We shut up, shut down, and shapeshift. Change and growth are a healthy pairing. But when the impulse to change comes from outside pressure or a place of inadequacy or shame, we're forced into a dysfunctional relationship with ourselves.

Sheri Swokowski wanted to change her voice to feel more

like herself. Swokowski is a former US Army colonel (now retired) and the highest-ranking transgender military officer ever. We sat together at her spotless dining room table, talking. After hiding her true self for decades, Swokowski was working as a lead instructor at Fort Belvoir, Virginia, when she transitioned.

"I decided to move and be authentic. I came out to my family, told the people at my force management school that I was going to take leave for six weeks and that I would be back as Sheri." When she returned to work, she was greeted first with the word "Welcome," then with the news that she'd been replaced. That moment helped turn Swokowski into the advocate for transgender rights she is today.

As a woman who transitioned from male to female, voice was one high-impact area where Swokowski chose to place her focus. "It really made me a little bit insecure when I was out in public that people would pick up on my voice being more masculine," she told me. To help herself feel more at ease, she spent a year in a voice program at George Washington University designed to help transgender individuals. She speaks today at a relaxed pace and comfortable pitch, at home with who and where she is.

"It's a big part of being authentic, and it's the only thing you can't really buy," Swokowski says of the voice. The question of authenticity, the right to speak as the person you are, is common to everyone. The voice that reflects your self isn't necessarily the voice you were born with. I believe it's simplistic to think otherwise.

Given the heavy lifting the voice does every day to express our sense of agency and self, it's imperative to build any changes we make to it upon a positive foundation. If you want to explore the full capacity of your voice for the joy of it or because you're motivated by its potential, then Godspeed. But if you're starting from a position of fear or shame, those issues must be resolved first, before you try to make any meaningful changes. Sometimes working with your voice can sweep away shame and move you toward a better relationship with yourself at the same time. My own work and experience coaching women has shown that while the issues surrounding the voice and authentic self can be complex, when we sit down to take self-inventory, we have an inner compass that tells us whether we truly want or need to do a rehab of the voice or just take it out for more joyrides. Our voice wants to tell us the truth.

CHANGE FROM WITHIN

Mary Edwards is a former military surgeon who spent years locked in a struggle with her own voice. Edwards, who graduated from West Point in 1992, retired after thirty years of service, with deployments in Iraq and Afghanistan. She had many posts over the years, including chief of pediatric surgery at Tripler Army Medical Center in Hawaii and general director of surgery at Baylor University in Texas. In 2014, she became general surgery consultant to the surgeon general, a post she held until her retirement.

Surgery is still a field dominated by men and an area famous for its high stakes and outsize egos. To some extent, surgeons hold life and death in their hands, a professional calling that some people claim requires unbecoming allowances of confidence and self-assurance. Critics call it a God complex. As more women enter the field, the culture in the OR may be changing, but to a certain extent, being a surgeon means being the voice in command. The role can be daunting for young women who grew up in a world that loves to praise quiet women.

Edwards told me it wasn't the professional culture she had found challenging; it was her internal struggle to lay claim to her voice.

"I used to be very meek and accommodating," she remembers. "I used to be obsessed with the idea that people would think I was bitchy or obnoxious or high maintenance. That was my problem. Once I decided it wasn't going to be a problem anymore, it was fine." In fact, it was more than fine, because in the OR, as in life, confidence pays off.

For ten years, Edwards struggled to overcome her fears about sounding too assertive. Finally the dam broke. Now Edwards is in charge, and she sounds it, but she does it her own way.

"I found that the people around you respond to confidence, and it was my issue with not being assertive and authoritative," she says. "People want the impression that whoever is captain of the ship knows what they're doing, so you have to be able to communicate effectively and with confidence." It took her ten years, but she finally moved into a voice with more confidence. In other words, she gave herself permission to sound like the skilled surgeon she was; she got into a position of alignment between self and self-expression. When you're ready for it, a change like this can feel like the sudden running of sap in spring; it can feel like power.

In surgery, as in many other high-intensity fields, there is such a thing as vocal destiny. Yes, vocal destiny sounds like a nineties boy band, but in this case it means that *you are perceived as you sound*. If I show up to work at a college bar with vocal fry, the trait may not cause so much as a ripple on the water, and it might even endear me to my coworkers. But if I work, and am trying to advance my career, in law, business, academia, politics, or broadcast news, my voice and the way I use it may matter more. The voice is part of the complete package, which includes your deftness as a communicator and your emotional intelligence. Doing a deep dive on where you are and where you're headed will yield dividends in self-knowledge, information that can help you act with intention and purpose as you hack your path through the thicket of life. No matter what you decide about your voice and how you'd like to use it, doing a little reflection on your journey is a task that can only help you take sure-footed steps as you go.

If You Feel Your Voice May Be Holding You Back, You Have Two Options.

1. Consider working with your voice to bring it into closer alignment with industry expectations. You will benefit from the chance to learn more about your voice and how to use it in new ways. If you do change your vocal style, be careful not to get stuck behind a plastic version of yourself and instead incorporate it into the person you are already, so that it amplifies your sense of self and personal power instead of masking it. If the journey is a good one, you'll learn something invaluable about how to play your instrument, which will allow you to play, create, and contribute in new ways. You can take this knowledge with you wherever you go, and it will change your life.

2. Do nothing. Maybe you work in a field where voice doesn't matter as much when weighed against other qualities. Maybe you love your voice exactly as it is, or maybe you'd like to help drive change and urge your colleagues to broaden the culture of acceptable voices and vocal styles. In that case, change nothing and stand strong.

CHAPTER 4

Always a Bridesmaid, Never the CEO of a Fortune 500 Company

"A udrey" was still a junior player in the world of bank regulation when she and her all-male team showed up to gather documentation for a case they were working on. The bank president walked into the conference room and brandished a folder in the air. "Here's the return. Who wants it?"

Of course, Audrey jumped right in. After all, this was why she was here, why she'd gone back to school to get that master's in public administration, and why she'd followed a gut-level calling all the way to a supremely male-dominated industry.

After graduation, MPA in hand, she'd landed her first job as a bank regulator in a large midwestern city, and here she was, doing the job she'd been preparing for since the beginning of the Great Recession. Watching the financial crisis unfold in slow-motion tidal waves of destruction, she began to listen to her gut. Quite persistently, it was telling her "You need to get in there, Audrey. This is your moment. You can help." She'd been dreaming of a job just like this one. It was an ideal match for her skill set, and she showed up to work well qualified and with optimism for miles.

"I would *love* to look it over!" Audrey replied. The bank president stopped and glanced over at her, maybe taking in the qualities she didn't think mattered when you worked hard and knew your stuff. She was young and female. "Sweetheart," he said, "you don't know how."

Audrey was livid. On the inside, that is. Her face went up in scalding ghost pepper flames. She knew she had more education than almost everybody else in the room, including the bank president. *I'm more qualified than you! I spent years in corporate tax work, I have my master's, and I'm older!* She didn't voice any of that out loud. Because at that moment, she made a choice: she said nothing at all.

Audrey is not a quiet woman. The first time we met in a workshop I was teaching, her strength and energy supercharged the air and made the room feel too small to contain her. She was confident, well connected, a devastatingly funny storyteller, and it was hard to imagine anyone shutting her down, but she showed up that April morning because she wasn't being heard and she'd had enough. Also because, one day at work, she had overheard two of her female colleagues talking about her— they'd thought Audrey was off the conference call, but she was there on the line, able to hear every word. One of them was talking up Audrey, but it didn't go down the way Audrey would have liked. "She really knows her stuff," said Audrey's booster, "but you have to get used to her voice. You know sexy baby voice? That's what she sounds like."

After reading about Margaret Thatcher's transformational elocution lessons, Audrey came to me hoping that a similar approach could help in her own professional life. More than anything else, she was ready to be taken seriously.

That day with the bank president is burned into Audrey's memory years later. It's not that she didn't take any action. Except for the heat in her face, she kept her composure in the moment and then brought the matter to her boss, a mild-mannered guy who didn't like to rock the boat.

"He's originally from the South," her boss said soothingly, as if growing up in proximity to high-quality fried chicken ex-plained everything. "It's a southern thing. Just get to know him a little." Audrey didn't believe it was a southern thing for a hot second, and in that moment she knew she was on her own.

Here's the thing: instead of being a one-and-done slight, however humiliating it might have been, that first encounter with the bank president set a *tone*. It was not a pleasant tone or a fleeting one but something as tangible as a palm on the cold side of a glass pane. She describes it as: "Nope. You're always gonna be out *there*. Not in the group with the guys."

Sometimes, in meetings, Audrey was so desperate to get her idea onto the board that beforehand, she'd ask a male colleague to propose it for her. The scenario became a real-life echo of the viral 1988 *Punch* cartoon in which a single woman is sitting in a boardroom with five men. A mustachioed fellow at the head of the table says, "That's an excellent suggestion, Miss Triggs. Perhaps one of the men here would like to make it."

Audrey knew that if a woman pitched an idea, it would never make it over the fence. When I wondered if she had ever considering asking a male colleague to back her up and amplify her voice instead of taking credit, she broke into laughter. "They'd never do it." So she forced herself to be content with getting her idea onto the floor.

In bank regulation, the ratio of the sexes was so tilted toward men that most of the time, Audrey was the only woman in the room. She wasn't the only woman to struggle with the gender dynamic. At the FDIC, she remembered, there was an older woman who wouldn't go to meetings anymore because the men in the room simply ignored her when she spoke. One day, she just stopped showing up. If you were young and made an effort with your appearance, if you wore enough makeup, the men would let you hang around, inspire them, and do double the work they did, Audrey recalled. If you were an older woman, though, it was twice as difficult, with almost no chance to make an impact. Audrey had had enough.

Earlier in her career, when men had explained things to her at length that she knew to be incorrect, she let them continue, assuming she must remind them of their daughter or granddaughter. But that got old, and Audrey stopped playing along. She was done keeping quiet, and she'd never been very good at it anyway. As the years wore on, she stopped listening patiently when someone tried to sell her a bad bill of goods. Instead, she just interrupted them, and said, "No, you're wrong. Here's why." Friends were concerned. "Why do you keep speaking up?" they asked her. "You're making it harder!"

Eventually she realized she'd hit the ceiling. "I can always get in the top three, but I can't be in charge. I can be a supporting player, but I can't get credit." So she made the decision to leave and focus on raising a family. "But I'll be back," she thought fiercely the whole time. "I'll be back." Today she's readying herself to run for political office.

Looking back on that early humiliation with the bank president, Audrey knows exactly what she'd do today. "I would have blown up the room," she says. "That's what has to happen. Pointing it out and pointing it out. It's exhausting and it's extra work, but that's how change happens. You have to stand up for yourself right away. You have to blow up the room." Women like Audrey are figuring out what works when their voices get squashed. Sometimes they wait it out; other times, they blow up the room.

The vocabulary of speaking while female is fun and breezy, but its real-world ramifications are not. Just ask Audrey. When a woman is denied the fullness of her voice—because it is ignored, ridiculed, or violently suppressed—there are consequences for families, careers, business outcomes, women themselves, and ultimately the uneasily steered course of a culture overly influenced by a monoculture of male voices.

Rebecca Solnit laid a cornerstone in the speaking-while-female structure with her essay "Men Explain Things to Me." The piece unpacked the experience of mansplaining from a woman's perspective, although the term never appears in her essay. In a 2012 piece reflecting on the influence of the writing, she said, "Having the right to show up and speak are basic to survival, to dignity and to liberty. I'm grateful that, after an early life of being silenced, sometimes violently, I grew up to have a voice, circumstances that will always bind me to the rights of the voiceless." That's the bedrock of the struggle for women and other historically silenced voices: to have a voice is to be given the right to thrive—at your job, in your relationships, as a citizen, and as a human being.

FOUNDING MOTHERS

Women today may not be entirely voiceless, but when we do speak, as we are wont to do, a shiver runs down the collective spine of Western civilization. The right to speak in public is one we assume was granted long ago, if ever we knew that once it was not. We remember the fight for the right to vote, suffragettes clad in white bearing sashes that read "Votes for Women," but the foundational battle that made it possible is largely forgotten. To truly understand where we are today, we need to understand where we've come from and why that journey isn't nearly as remote as we may think.

When women fought to participate in the antislavery movement in the late 1830s and 1840s, they faced fierce opposition, first on the grounds that it was inappropriate for women to be involved in public affairs, then on the basis that it was unseemly for women to address men, and ultimately on the premise that it was impermissible for women to speak in public at all. Pioneers such as Lucy Stone and Angelina Grimké persevered, however.

Lucy Stone knew she wanted to be a public speaker when she was twenty-eight years old, although to do so was to stare down the disapproving barrel of society. She was the first woman from Massachusetts to earn a college degree, and even before her name was linked to abolitionist and women's rights causes, she turned down Oberlin College when it offered her the chance to write a commencement speech that she wouldn't be allowed to deliver because she was a woman. At the time, women at Oberlin could debate one another in their own company, but female rhetoric students were supposed to learn by watching men practice. But Stone was such a badass that she and a friend formed a women's off-campus debate club to hone their skills, then circled back and won the opportunity to conduct a women-only debate in front of the full class. The event was such a success and drew such a large crowd that Oberlin faculty responded by banning women's oral exercises in coed classes altogether.

Still, public speaking was a calling for Stone, and her voice broke through. After graduation, she began writing and delivering speeches for the American Anti-Slavery Society. Even though she was heckled and once physically attacked by a mob, she was undeterred and built a reputation for being a master storyteller with the ability to hold audiences spellbound. She went on to tour the United States and Canada as an orator on the subject of abolition and women's rights, and made more money at it than many of her male colleagues did. In 1850, her speech at the first National Woman's Rights Convention in Worcester, Massachusetts (which she herself organized), was reprinted in newspapers around the world.

Angelina Grimké is another pioneer who helped win the right for women to speak in public. Grimké grew up part of a slave-owning family on a plantation in South Carolina, where the cruelty and inequality she witnessed compelled her to take action. She and her sister Sarah were among the first women to speak in public against slavery, and their talks drew criticism from men and women alike, along with disapproval from some ministers for their "unwomanly behavior." If the response sounds mild, Grimké once spoke at an antislavery convention in Philadelphia and later that same night, an angry mob burned the building to the ground. Grimké went on to become the first woman in the country to address a lawmaking body.

Like Stone and Grimké, Sojourner Truth is a luminary in the historic struggle to bring women's voices to public spaces. A formerly enslaved person, she couldn't read or write, but even so, she developed a powerful personal voice that captured her unique sensibility of the world. Her most remarkable and celebrated speech was delivered extemporaneously at the 1851 Women's Rights Convention in Akron, Ohio. Truth went on to a successful career as a public speaker on the subject of women's rights and the abolition movement.

Long before Stone, Truth, and Grimké, Aristotle pondered the qualities of slaves, women, and men in his *Politics*. "As the poet says, 'Silence is a woman's glory,' but this is not equally the glory of man," he concluded. This ideology has some company. In I Corinthians, the apostle Paul wrote, "Women should remain silent in the churches. They are not allowed to speak but must be in submission."

The biblical ideal of a silent, submissive woman is surprisingly persistent. But it isn't unique to the history of Christianity, Congress, or the Roman Forum. Its overtones still reverberate today when women are ignored, interrupted, or criticized for the timbre of their voices. Or when their stories are dismissed and pushed to the margins. When women comprise only

5 percent of CEOs in the Fortune 500 in 2018; when men
dominate the highest court in the land and both chambers
of Congress. When the phrase "ice pick in your ear" is used
on cable TV to describe a female politician's voice. It's not a
stretch to draw a line from ancient Rome and the New Tes-
tament all the way through to the women's suffragist leader
Susan B. Anthony and end up at Hillary Clinton in the year
2016.

Looking back at the early struggles for women's rights
in a piece she wrote for the *Independent* in 1900, Anthony
said, "No advanced step taken by women has been so bitterly
contested as that of speaking in public. For nothing which
they have attempted, not even to secure the suffrage, have
they been so abused, condemned and antagonized." She recalled the amazement of the first female organizers in the
temperance movement who, having been invited to attend
the men's temperance convention, found they were expected
only to "listen and learn, not speak." When these women
tried to make the case for more, they were "literally howled
down with cries of 'Shame, shame!'" In other words, American society was more enraged about letting women speak in
public than it was about giving them the right to vote. It's
an extraordinary statement that explains a lot about why,
in a moment of growing awareness about society's current
inequities, women's voices are still challenged in the last
citadels of male-dominated power. It also makes one thing
clear: women's voices aren't simply a means to grasp power
and change; women's voices *are* power.

POWER RANKING

Yet even with that knowledge in hand, women's voices are far from fully heard. Evidence shows that for women, closing the talking gap is tough and nowhere near as simple to resolve as it may sound. In 2011, Victoria Brescoll from Yale University's School of Management wanted to know how much powerful women talked compared with men of equal power. She began by looking at the US Senate, which has two qualities that make it ideal for study: first, every word is recorded, and second, senators are some of the most powerful people in US politics. Brescoll zoomed in on gender, how much time was spent speaking on the Senate floor, and what was called a "power score," a measure of various factors combined to assess a senator's clout.

She found that male senators with high power scores spent more time talking on the Senate floor than male senators with lower power scores. But for women, there was no direct relationship between high power and time spent talking. In other words, heavy-hitting male senators spoke more than their colleagues of lower rank, but high-powered female senators didn't see the same floor time boost.

After that initial experiment, Brescoll took a different approach to the same question. She instructed both men and women participants to imagine themselves as both the most and the least powerful members in a team meeting at work, then asked them how much time they would expect to spend talking in that scenario. Men reported that they would spend more time talking if they held a position of power and less time talking if not. But women reported no difference in talk time, regardless of their power status. What's more, deeper digging found that the high-power women adjusted their talking time for fear of being seen as controlling or "out of line." They were the only ones to do so. This is important because it tells us not simply that women choose to speak less than men at work, but also that they do so out of fear.

Finally, Brescoll had study participants rate hypothetical male and female CEOs. In that scenario, subjects judged a female executive who talked more than her peers as less suited for the job. Her competency rating went down by 14 percent. But a male executive who did the same thing enjoyed a sweet 10 percent rating surge.

Brescoll's study shows that women who shy away from talking too much on the job for fear of a social backlash may be right to worry. If men assert their voices on the job, they appear more likely to be clapped on the back and given a promotion, whereas a woman who does the same thing may find herself sinking to the bottom of the hierarchy, right behind the guy who microwaves fish for lunch in the communal break room.

Though you are unlikely to find yourself on a hiring committee where candidate evaluations include the critique "Talks too much!," a dominant workplace culture with an implicit bias favoring men who speak up and speak often and that penalizes women who do the same is in effect a culture that silences women and keeps them from participating fully in their professional lives and the greater work ecosystem.

You may never hear anyone voicing the belief that a woman at work should speak less, but you may hear words such as *aggressive*, *harsh*, *bitchy*, or *abrasive* instead. Or you may see invisible signs of disapproval, like a colleague who is bypassed for promotion, ignored, or laughed at behind her back. These are all coded ways to say the same thing women have been hearing for hundreds and hundreds of years: keep it down, ladies.

Brescoll's findings are important evidence of the nearly impossible-to-prove inklings that women have had over the decades, the sense that when they talk, something isn't right. Instead of coding the disapproving response as gender related or outright sexism, women have personalized and internalized the resulting backlash and gone silent. Over the years, we've thought: my idea didn't cut it, I'm not funny, I'm unlikable, I must sound like an idiot, I'm in over my head, I don't know what I'm talking about.

Now we know better. Sure, sometimes our idea might not be the right one. But other times, when we feel like Ingrid Bergman in *Gaslight*, that's because we are. At those moments when you know your idea is strong and your presentation knocked it out of the park but nobody's listening, it can be a profound comfort to tell yourself: it might not be me.

It's worth pausing a moment to remember that in Brescoll's study, women tended to stay quiet out of fear. Anytime fear enters the talking equation, we should send out warning flares, because silence and fear have no place in our culture or in the workplace and fly in the face of societal ideals of egalitarianism and democratic participation.

THE REAL MEANING OF A VOICE AT THE TABLE

I've never liked people who stare. When I was a teenager in a restaurant, I would give babies the stink eye if they clambered up to a standing position in the booth next to ours and gazed over the edge at me in that unblinking way toddlers have. Only later in life did I realize that it was possible to hunger for eye contact as affirmation that I had been seen, that I'd been heard, and that I was important enough to share a visual connection with, if only for a moment.

Early in my career, a puzzling series of meetings with two male colleagues brought the issue into focus. One attendee happened to be a coworker who was also a friend; the other, a straight-up colleague. Somewhere along the way, I realized that even when the conversation directly affected me, the colleague's comments were directed to my friend. As was all of the eye contact.

I would give my opinion, raise questions, and do everything but hire a marching band to highlight my point, but the colleague never made eye contact with me, save in chance, fleeting moments, after which his eyes locked back onto my friend, like a compass returning to north.

As often happens with women, my thoughts spiraled downward. At first I thought I must be paranoid: Why is he avoiding my eyes? What does he know that I don't? Then I questioned my professional effectiveness. And then, as the dismal meetings continued unchanged, I became discouraged. I considered a friend who'd just made the leap from music composition to food science. Perhaps I would follow suit, give up the media altogether, and begin a thoughtful, quiet career in poultry science, where the chickens would have no choice but to regard me with beady-eyed respect.

Each individual meeting stung a little, but the cumulative effect was greater. I tried a different approach. I prepared feverishly each morning before we met and came prepared to shoehorn my way in, like a losing contestant on *The Bachelor*. I laughed extra hard at jokes, and when that didn't work, I simply interrupted and wrested control of the conversation. But ownership lasts only as long as you keep talking, and unless you're wearing a catheter and have hours to kill on the Senate floor, eventually you have to stop.

At last, after the latest bruising session, I turned to my friend and said, "I have to tell you something."

He was skeptical at first, and, being the kind of person who, quite reasonably, wanted proof, he set out to see for himself.

"I'll pay attention the next time," he agreed. And he did.

The next time we met, my friend waited until we had the room to ourselves, then looked me in the eye and said, "You're right, he absolutely will not look at you." I noted the touch of incredulity in his voice with satisfaction. The vindication felt good, and even better, there was now another person aware of the dynamic, so I wasn't alone on my puny, eye-contactless island.

The next time we met, my friend and ally said pointedly, "Veronica's got this one," and looked right at me. It was the verbal equivalent of a baton handoff, designed to highlight my role and signal my inclusion in the discussion. In a perfect world, that would have done the trick, but despite the clear verbal cue, the colleague gave me a quick nod and turned back to my friend.

In response, my ally swiveled his chair off to an oblique angle and began scanning the papers in front of him, deliberately refusing to look up.

Our colleague faltered a bit but kept talking, clearly waiting for my friend to resume the conversation and the eye contact.

Eventually, when glance after glance to his usual target went unmet, his eyes settled on mine, and for the first meeting I could remember, he looked at me as we spoke.

Being heard in the workplace is about more than talking while other people listen; it's the accumulated weight of intangibles such as eye contact, body language, power and influence, interruptions, and idea-poaching or praise. Looking back at those meetings, there might have been a million reasons why I wasn't given the same clout as my friend. Maybe our coworker held my friend's judgment in especially high regard, maybe he was more comfortable talking to a man or more uncomfortable talking with me. Or maybe he simply didn't realize he was shutting me out. It's hard to know, but my experience is far from unusual.

Although there are no longer large, organized social movements bent solely on silencing women, the living shadow of those sentiments still makes it hard for women to speak today.

In 2014, then Uber board member David Bonderman said that if Uber's board had more women, it would mean "more talking." Considering the company's reputation for being unfriendly toward women, it perhaps came as no surprise that Bonderman relied on the old sexist trope that women chatter a lot without saying much. He later resigned after his remarks drew an outcry, but not before exposing the outdated scaffolding of a system that privileges male voices. Men enjoy more perceived power than women when they speak and more authority, and they are more likely to be able to speak unencumbered by interruptions or skepticism.

HOW TO CLOSE THE TALKING GAP

The talking gap between men and women is real. Here's the rub: sometimes words are airy nothings that fill time and evaporate with the first gust of wind; other times they represent weight, power, and influence. The women I work with are clear: they don't want to speak just to hear themselves talking. They're not interested in wasting time and learning to pontificate on demand; posturing and peacocking hold little appeal for them. What they're looking for is not just a seat at the table but a voice and the chance to make a difference.

In 2012, the journal *American Political Science Review* published a study by political scientists who asked the questions "What happens to women's voices and authority during deliberative discussions?" and "What changes based on the gender composition of the group?" Christopher Karpowitz, Tali Mendelberg, and Lee Shaker recruited participants, both men and women, to have group discussions about a made-up scenario: how to distribute the money they earned together from tasks they were told they'd be doing later in the experiment.

Here's what they found: in deliberative bodies that used "majority rule"—that is, the yielding of complete decision-making authority to the largest group—when men greatly outnumbered women, there was a sizable talking gap. The smaller numbers of women stayed quiet. Women, the researchers found, typically talked less than 75 percent of the time that men talked, in proportion to their representation. What's more, in these decision-making bodies, the researchers concluded, talking itself translated to authority and clout within the group—which meant that women were in the position of lesser power. When women in male-majority groups did speak, they were less likely to be rated as influential overall. Follow-up analysis found that they were also more likely to face hostile interruptions.

In short, this is the exact same setup we see today in board-rooms around the world, although the numbers show the needle is now moving in the right direction. In 2017, women accounted for 38 percent of incoming board directors, a notable increase from the year before. Women held 14.7 percent of the seats on boards in 2015, according to a Credit Suisse review of three thousand global companies. This is encouraging change but far from parity.

At first glance, the deliberative discussion research paints a demoralizing scenario: put a couple of women at the table with a big group of guys, and they'll talk less than the men and have little sway over what decision finally shoots out the other end. But wait—there's a catch, and it's an important one. When one of two things happened, women's voices caught up to men's in power, influence, and respect. The first tweak that worked for women was switching to consensus-building discussions—that is, to unanimous rule where everyone must agree on the outcome. The other change that worked for women was to increase the number of women in the group to make up 80 percent of the total group. When either of those things happened—voilà!—women's voices were heard.

Of significance, women's voices changed the game. When women participated equally in the discussion, the groups ar-rived at different decisions; women swung the group. "When women participated more, they brought unique and helpful perspectives to the issue under discussion," Karpowitz said. "We're not just losing the voice of someone who would say the same things as everybody else in the conversation."

It may not be feasible to rule by consensus in every situation, but the findings of Karpowitz, Mendelberg, and Shaker offer demonstrable proof that if organizations care about giving women a voice at the table, they can put their practice where their HR is. As the researchers suggested, the group moderator could begin by stating that the group wishes to hear from every individual at the table and making a "no interruptions" rule.

Another technique that works well for women in group settings is to amplify one another's voices, especially if the gender balance tips toward men. If a woman at a meeting isn't being heard, women—and men—can refer back to her thoughts and give them more weight. It's as simple as saying, for example, "I liked what Meeshay said about our priorities. She's on the right track." If you have no allies in the room, another way to reclaim an idea is by using a technique like the one from public television executive Deanna Mackey. She uses the deft "I'm glad you picked up on my point, Dan" to draw a line of ownership back to herself.

When in the early days of the Obama administration women found themselves in the minority (with men installed in two-thirds of the top aide positions), they made a deliberate choice to make amplification of one another's voices and ideas a routine working habit. It was a strategy that had a dual purpose of amping up women's contributions in the present moment and changing the culture around gender-influenced communication at the same time.

When the voices of women and other marginalized people are sidelined, it's not merely a nuisance and a petty hurt. It means the loss of talent and the perpetuation of unnaturally tilted organizations. After months or sometimes years of struggling to be heard and respected, many women decide there's no point fighting gravity, so they quit. Like Audrey, they leave to start a family or they move on, seeking a friendlier climate for women, contributing to the industry-wide erosion of talent pools.

When it comes to whether or not we hear women's voices clearly and organizations and individuals value what women bring to the table, climate matters. Having more women at the table means a dynamic shift for other women and the opportunity for new through roads for underrepresented voices in general: of women, people of color, and non-cisgender people.

Watch carefully. What happens at your company when a woman speaks more loudly, more directly, or at greater length than other women, or men? Is she rewarded or penalized? Does she get interrupted or ignored? Does her career trajectory take off or stall out? And a bigger question: Are there women at your company to open the door for other underrepresented voices and to model active, verbal participation? While we spin our wheels and muse about what it means to listen to women's voices, we already have good data to act upon. In the workplace, companies can begin to urge verbal participation by everyone at the table. This practice will normalize the sound of women talking alongside men for all genders and has the potential to shift workplace culture and, by extension, society in general. We can also work seriously toward hiring equal numbers of men and women, when possible, to create a friendly or even neutral environment for women to speak in. Finally, when conditions allow, we can move toward a consensus-building model of decision-making when women are in the minority, to help surface women's voices during deliberative discussions. These are straightforward, cost-effective strategies that can help bring women's perspectives to the table, and research shows what comes next could change the game for everyone.

SEEING IS BELIEVING

George Dawes Green is the founder of the hit storytelling show *The Moth*. Along the way, he's learned some important lessons about what it takes to surface women's voices and what women themselves need in order to speak.

The Moth is now a public radio show, a stage performance, a podcast, and a book. In an interview on Wisconsin Public Radio's *Central Time*, Green told me about what it took to get women up onstage, telling their stories:

> *When we first started our* Moth *slams, our amateur slams . . . back in 2000 . . . those are nights when people*

*come and put their name in a hat, and your name is picked
and you get a score and you can win the slam and go on to
the grand slam. You can become famous through this process. Originally it was only men who would do it. Women
would not tell stories. You know, we did everything we
could, and we could get one woman a night who would invariably tell a soft, gentle story and would lose. And so this
happened for several years. . . . Some people were saying,
maybe, you know, men were just better storytellers than
women. And then slowly women began to get up and tell
stories. And other women sort of saw, oh, I can do that,
too. And now we've had, just in the last fifteen years, this
incredible transformation. The majority of our storytellers
are now women, and they win the majority of the slams
and the grand slams. . . . It just took . . . these nights, and it
took women kind of seeing that there was a template.*

Women need to see other women speaking, telling stories,
serving on boards, participating fully and out loud. And when
women do share their voices, other women need to see them
being respected for it, given promotions, approval, and genuine consideration. For decades, women have governed their
voices in relation to cultural dog whistles of disapproval, pun-
ishment, and shame. We have heard that our voices sound
wrong or annoying, that we don't have an equal right to be
heard or to participate in civic and professional life. We know
better now, and as a society, we know what we need to do to
give women's voices an equal shot.

THE TYRANNY OF OPEN OFFICE PLANS

Along with being on the lookout for self-silencing and bias, there are other, less obvious ways to close the talking gap at work. "Renee" came to me hoping to uncover a stronger voice and increased speaking confidence. As is often the case with the women I work with, there was a powerful male figure at work who made it challenging for her to speak.

Renee was successful at her job and the leader of a team but faltered during moments when it was her turn to sell her team's achievements and tell a compelling story. Our goal was to help her command the room when she spoke at meetings, and to paint a vivid picture of all she'd accomplished.

Renee was confident and sure of the value of her work, but when it came time to telegraph that confidence, her voice told a different story. It sounded fatigued and had a hushed quality. As we worked our way through some beginning vocal exercises, I couldn't shake the feeling that it was almost as though she was speaking in a stage whisper instead of at full voice, even when the moment demanded it. She had a large vocal range and had no trouble moving comfortably through her register during vocal exercises, with a little coaching.

At one of our sessions together, I asked her, "Does anyone ever tell you that you have a soft voice?" She looked surprised, thought about the question for a moment, and told me no. We went back to the drawing board. But the next week she came back and said, "I talked to my husband and he said he has trouble hearing me a lot of the time and pointed out that my mother—who's getting older—can almost never hear me."

Renee wasn't old enough to have the vocal strength declines that can come with advanced age, and she didn't have a high-voice-demand job, like a teacher or a trainer. Questions like this one are thorny. How do our vocal habits develop the way they do and why? In this way, digging back through the past can be a bit like therapy.

Even when there may not be one lightning-strike moment that forever shapes our relationship with our voice, we tend to internalize the environment around us, and the childhood script of the good, quiet girl is hard to shake. As Renee and I scoured her life for possible root causes of her present-day voice, I had a sudden inspiration. "Do you happen to work in an open office plan?" I asked her. Bingo.

Though, as a manager, Renee had an office of her own, she spent much of her day among the cubicles, talking with the members of her team, and she consciously lowered her voice to speak with them, so as not to disturb anyone. She did so all day long, forty-plus hours a week. She showed me her office; it was a beautiful modern space, but it was typical of cubicle work today: every noise exposed, little privacy, and what I now believe is one of the most challenging environ-ments for women. Today, newly constructed open-concept offices often come with a white-noise component, but whether or not that's enough to override the deeply ingrained response many women have to manifest qualities of consideration and thoughtfulness by anticipating colleagues' need for quiet remains to be seen.

Having been conditioned from a young age to understand that to be a good girl is to be undisruptive and that it is a woman's job to be finely attuned to those around her, many women wilt in open office plans, scurrying around apologetically with ducked heads and hunched shoulders.

For my client, the whispered communication day after day after day had taken its toll, and she had begun to carry that half voice with her home from the office. Her voice had become a shadow of itself, and Renee had become unaccustomed to the sound of robust, unshackled speech.

Renee was the first woman to come to me with cubicle voice, but she wasn't the last. Each time I meet a new client with a hushed, whispery voice, the first thing I ask her to do is describe her work environment. Most of the time, she works in an open office. Admittedly, men also work in open office plans and calibrate their voices on the job accordingly, but because they aren't bombarded with the constant messaging about the desirability of being quiet, they seem to be better able to shrug off the work voice once they step out the office door. Based on my experience, women appear more likely to incorporate it into their larger lives and have a harder time speaking at full strength later, whether at home or in the boardroom.

CUBICLE VOICE: LOOKING FOR SOLUTIONS

We can support one another in the quest for robust speaking voices, no matter what the office environment. One approach is to have a discussion about the problem. As companies look to invest in the women on staff and ready them for greater responsibility and leadership, voice matters. Understanding that cubicle work can have a chilling effect on the voice and general demeanor of women in the office, women's resource groups can create a culture that rewards women for taking up space with their voices, and women in positions of influence can set an example of inhabiting their role publicly with a strong voice.

Today, many open-concept offices have breakout rooms, where groups of staffers can go for privacy or small-group work. Women can use these rooms frequently during the day and think of them as voice-training rooms where their voice can be used to its full potential, without fear of disturbing anyone deep in concentration, just as lunch groups meet to practice meditation or do yoga.

Workplaces that want to support women's voices can also cultivate a culture where a little hubbub is acceptable. Instead of piping in white noise and installing sound baffles—or at least in addition to those measures—companies can buy everyone a pair of noise-canceling headphones to put on when they need to hunker down. They can also make it clear that it's not a crime against humanity to have a voice that carries, particularly for women. Organizations could also consider designating certain areas as "quiet zones," like study carrel rooms at universities, for workers in need of deep quiet. That way, a woman working to develop or maintain a confident, powerful voice won't be swimming against the tide every day in the office and there will be clearly delineated quiet areas to reduce the potential for noise-related workplace dust-ups.

If you diagnose yourself with a bad case of cubicle voice, don't forget that the story doesn't begin and end with how you sound. Remember, the voice is housed in the body and is, in many ways, a reflection of the body's relative well-being. When we feel self-conscious and fearful—in this case, about being loud and inconsiderate—our bodies reflect that state; we tend to stoop over, hunch our shoulders, and tip our chin toward our chest in a self-protective manner, as though preparing to scoot through a battlefield without being seen by enemy archers. Whether we're cognizant of it or not, this is a defensive state of being that can produce corresponding negative thoughts that in turn manifest in behaviors we'd rather not have. No one is promoted for being furtive and good at scuttling.

Renee and I worked together to bring out the fullest, strongest version of her voice. She also switched jobs. We met recently, and her voice and confidence were on full display; she'd ditched the cubicle whisper and was using a strong, ringing voice. Later we traded some thoughts about the change, and she told me that she'd paid her old office a visit recently. "I was surprised to find that my throat actually hurt and felt strained by the time I left. Even after we worked together . . . it was hard to break the habit and not feel like I was disturbing my coworkers. So my voice was raspy or hoarse a lot of the time." She went on, "In my current office layout, office suites with a central work area, I do speak at full volume throughout the day. And at the end of the day, my voice doesn't feel strained. I give a lot of short presentations to leadership, and my full voice—that is not strained or achy—reflects the confidence that I feel."

Renee's story has a happy ending that took awareness-building and a change of environment. But her experience also raises an important point: whispering is hard on the voice; in fact, it can put more wear on the voice than speaking at a louder pitch level. In 2006, a hundred-person study conducted by Dr. Robert T. Sataloff (who is also an operatic baritone) at the Drexel University College of Medicine and Dr. Adam D. Rubin of the Lakeshore Professional Voice Center in St. Clair Shores, Michigan, used a fiber-optic scope to check out the vocal cords of subjects while they counted from one to ten, first in a normal voice, then in a whisper. They found that a large majority of people—sixty-nine—stressed their vocal cords by whispering. Dr. Rubin told the *New York Times*, "They were squeezing their vocal cords together more tightly to produce the whisper, which is more traumatic." Only thirteen people's voices responded to whispering with less stress.

Whether women are explicitly told to keep their voices down or not, workplaces have an important opportunity to support them with workplace cultures and structural models—sometimes literally from the ground up.

Talking Back to Cubicle Voice

1. Grab a yoga mat or blanket and the heaviest book you own. Think a Nordic cooking compendium or unabridged dictionary.

2. Lie on your back on the mat or blanket with your knees bent.

3. Place the heavy book on your lower abdomen.

4. Take a moment to imagine that you are introducing yourself at the World Economic Forum in Davos, Switzerland. You are the most powerful person in attendance, and everyone already knows who you are, but for formality's sake, you will need to introduce yourself anyway. Now do it!

5. It will be harder to speak lying down with a weight on your stomach; you'll need to engage the muscles that produce a strong voice. Use the weight to your advantage, and really let it rip. Don't push from the throat but from the lower abdomen, the seat of vocal power.

6. Not feeling it? Buddy up and have a partner push down on the book. Start gently and instruct the other person to add pressure if you need a little extra resistance to free the voice. Always be mindful of how your body and back feel during this exercise, and lighten up or stop if you're feeling any discomfort.

7. Practice! Do this exercise each morning, and try your hardest to port this voice into the workday with you. If you absolutely must whisper, set a reminder on your phone to turn off cubicle voice the moment you step out of the office.

8. Make some noise!

CHAPTER 5

Her, Interrupted

I n 2017, Democratic senator Elizabeth Warren became an icon for women's voices. While reading a letter by Coretta Scott King on the Senate floor, Warren was hit with the speaking-while-female trifecta: interruption, censure, and silencing. She was first interrupted midspeech and charged with violating a Senate rule in her critique of then attorney general nominee Jeff Sessions. Republican majority leader Mitch McConnell cited the rather obscure Rule 19 to silence Warren, and the Senate voted along party lines to forbid her from speaking for the remainder of the debate. In defense of his motion, McConnell uttered these now-famous words of censure:

Sen. Warren was giving a lengthy speech. She had appeared to violate the rule. She was warned. She was given an explanation. Nevertheless, she persisted.

A split second later, Twitter grabbed the baton and turned "Nevertheless, she persisted" into a battle cry. The phrase went viral, splashing onto bumper stickers, T-shirts, and hashtags associated with the feminist movement. It's even inspired the title of a children's book by Chelsea Clinton and Alexandra Boiger, *She Persisted: 13 American Women Who Changed the World.* Warren went on to read King's letter in its entirety outside the Senate chamber in a Facebook video, which was viewed more than 13 million times.

It's difficult to influence a conversation when you can't finish voicing a complete thought. Yet that's how women function in the world today. Ever socialized to be accommodating team players who listen attentively, women are often interrupted and silenced as a matter of course. Because this happens so often, we are not, by and large, accustomed to breaking in during a conversation or refusing to yield the floor when we ourselves are interrupted, even in high-stakes situations. Because of this, free-for-all, shout-it-out, elbow-in discussions are tough, but there are techniques every woman should have in her tool kit that can help.

Although I was a quiet kid who needed an engraved invitation to speak in class, today I'm at my best in a happy hubbub. I thrive on conversation that zips and zings, I enjoy peaks and valleys, overlapping voices, spontaneous jokes, quick laughter, and expressions of genuine feeling. A natural part of conversation is interrupting. There is a time and place for luxurious, slow, considered conversations, and this style is infinitely valuable, but if geologic discourse is your only setting, it may be time to experiment with a few new speeds.

Let's think of conversation as a rewarding game of basketball. Words are the ball, and the conversation is the game. It's bad form to hog the ball. It's also bad form to avoid taking the ball altogether or to get mad when someone steals it. Passing is good, as is cheering in the form of active listening. The three-pointer of the contribution itself isn't so much the goal as is the simple act of playing.

Men have long been granted the place of privilege in the game. They're the guards, the forwards, the centers. In life, as in the high school gym classes I remember, women are rarely given the ball, by anyone. They're not very likely to grab it, either, because when they do, there is often a price. And that's a shame. We'll never know the full cost of the ideas that go unsaid, the voices that are pushed aside, and the silent half-life of professional investment. But we can measure the phenomenon of interruptions to help us get real about what it's like for women when they talk.

According to a 2014 study by researchers at George Washington University, women are interrupted more often than men. The researchers set up three-minute conversations with volunteers—twenty were men and twenty were women. Each volunteer was paired with a conversational partner of either gender, and the topic was gender neutral—in this case, cell phone use and reality TV. I doubt you'll be surprised to find out that women were interrupted more often than men. But here's the kicker: women were interrupted more often both by men *and* by other women. Women interrupted men once per three-minute conversation but interrupted other women almost three times as often—2.8 times, to be exact. As for men, they interrupted their male conversational partner about 2 times and their female partner 2.6 times.

This poses the question, why are women more likely to interrupt other women? Both men and women may be more likely to perceive male figures as powerful. In that case, for either gender, it's less risky to interrupt a woman of perceived lower power than it is to interrupt a man. Women, then, are at the low end of the pecking order for *everybody*.

Beyond that, power in most organizations is concentrated at the top, and that power is overwhelmingly male. As women vie among themselves for positions of influence, they may look around and see only one or two spots at the top for women, setting the stage for a mentality of scarcity to develop. In that kind of climate, women may be more likely to be herded into positions of mutual competition rather than mutual advocacy. We should also consider the possibility that women interrupt other women more often than they interrupt men because it's safer. It may be that we'd actually *like* to bust in and get our thoughts onto the board, but the gendered rules of engagement are holding us back.

In any case, interruptions are a fact of life for women in the workplace. Some of us are more comfortable with interrupting or asserting ourselves to hold the floor, while others of us struggle to find our footing when we feel we could be interrupted at any moment. In response, some of us turn into a runaway train, exhaling words in a rush to get them all out in a hurry. Other times, the threat of interruption shakes our confidence, and we clam up.

Learning how to interrupt and how *not* to be interrupted are flip sides of the same coin. You need to know how to do both. This isn't to say that you need to make yourself over in the image of Walter "Shut the f*#@! up, Donny!" Sobchak from *The Big Lebowski*, but gaining a basic comfort level here can up your confidence and get you ready for anything that comes.

How you respond to interruptions will vary according to your conversational style, your environment, and whether or not you're having a damn-the-torpedoes kind of day. In my Speaking While Female workshops, I always schedule time to practice the skill of interrupting—because if you can't do it with your family on a Friday night when you desperately want to chime in with a vote for your favorite pizza place for dinner, it's not going to happen when the chips are down at work and your boss is in the room. Yes, some of us have been raised to consider it rude to interrupt and unseemly to wrangle the conversation back when you've been interrupted, but until you're CEO and run the whole show, it's a must-have skill in your tool kit, whether you use these techniques once an hour or once a year. Remember, it's okay to feel insecure about interrupting, and one day you will even learn to manage that discomfort; that comes with time. Eventually you may stop feeling uncomfortable altogether. But in the meantime, the feeling doesn't mean you're doing it wrong. Even former secretary of state Madeleine Albright said, "To this day, I sometimes feel a squirm of anxiety when I interrupt a discussion in a room with only men."

Based on what research tells us, men with more power are encouraged to speak at length, while women—both with power and without—are encouraged to zip it. This encouragement can arrive in subtle form, but nevertheless, it's there. For women, it's a fight for each word.

This is why cutting in during a conversation feels so alien; when women interrupt, we're breaking a social contract. The contract tells us that it's okay to participate, just not too much; to add our voice but to yield the floor to the most powerful person in the room. Interrupting is an assertion of influence and personal power, and assertions of power are a tough sell for women at work. Power dynamics like this may weigh especially heavy on young women and people of color, whose voices face even greater challenges in the world.

But until the prevailing culture of communication is no longer built upon a masculine, power-based example, getting comfortable with interruptions is one way for women to insist upon their right to speak. Though it won't remake the entire male-dominated communication culture itself, interrupting is an act of self-confidence and even subversion. Just ask the women on the Supreme Court.

At Northwestern University's Pritzker School of Law, Tonja Jacobi and Dylan Schweers wanted to see if women on the Supreme Court were less likely to be interrupted than other women. They wondered, could power give women immunity?

To get a handle on how often female Supreme Court justices were interrupted when compared with their male colleagues, Jacobi and Schweers examined fifteen years of transcripted arguments from the Court. Instead of finding evidence for the deference you might expect toward a Supreme Court justice, a position of immense esteem in our society, the researchers found the opposite. Even within the Supreme Court of the United States, women were interrupted far more than men during oral arguments—about three times as often. Jacobi and Schweers also discovered women were less likely to be the ones doing the interrupting—again, about three times less likely on average. And as the number of women on the Court increased over the years, so did the number of times women were interrupted. Even in the nation's highest court, women's voices were not granted equal respect.

And things aren't getting better as the Court approaches gender equity. The year 2015 marked the high point for "manterruptions" on SCOTUS, with Justice Elena Kagan interrupted ten times or more by male justices Samuel Alito, Anthony Kennedy, and John Roberts. Justice Sonia Sotomayor was interrupted fifteen times by Justice Kennedy, fourteen times by Justice Alito, and twelve times by Justice Roberts. And Justice Kennedy interrupted Justice Ruth Bader Ginsburg eleven times. To aggravate the issue, in 2015, interruptions of Justice Sotomayor by male attorneys arguing before the court accounted for a shocking 8 percent of all interruptions. Sotomayor is the only justice of color, hinting that race or ethnicity *and* gender are likely in play. With numbers like that, the 2015 spike in manterruptions provides possible evidence of a male pushback against growing gender equity on the Court.

Beyond interruptions among the justices themselves, advocates before the Court interrupted women justices more than they did men justices, which is not only a violation of SCOTUS rules but also an example of what researchers see as tangible evidence of missing deference.

So what happens when you're relatively new on the Court, you're a woman, and you keep getting interrupted? The answer is telling. In response to the frequent interruptions, Jacobi and Schweers found that over time, the female Supreme Court justices changed the way they spoke. For example, instead of gift wrapping their statements in "goodwill sandwiches," with formal acknowledgments like "Mr." or "Ms." and phrases such as "Excuse me," "Sorry," and "May I ask," the women justices began to speak more like the men. It seemed as though the polite language of their earlier days might have opened the door for interruptions. Here's an example:

RUTH BADER GINSBURG: Mr. Paden, because—
ANTHONY M. KENNEDY: I have one . . . one small
procedural question. Why is Dole properly before us? I
want to make you feel welcome here, but . . .

The longer they serve on the court, the more women justices learn to talk like the guys. They cut right to the chase
and jump in without hesitation in a markedly more abrupt
style. Female Supreme Court justices learn to break the social
contract that keeps women quiet and compliant.

But as Jacobi points out, interruptions are more than a
yardstick of civility; they are a measure of power, respect,
and influence. The oral arguments Jacobi studied are important.
They impact the decisions that have the power to remold
American life, so having their voice heard there matters very
much for women on the Court.

Though there is a "likely learning-curve" cost for newer
women on SCOTUS, their adaptation signals a willingness
to engage in and to claim ground for the full complement of
perspectives on the court. If their voices were silenced, verdicts
would be decided by the few instead of the many, and the
individual contributions of unique legal minds would be lost
to history.

Even women in Congress who win the right to be in the room
where it happens don't always have full speaking privileges.
First-year senator Kamala Harris, a former defense attorney

from California, made headlines in 2017 when she was repeatedly interrupted during her rapid-fire questioning of Deputy Attorney General Rod J. Rosenstein and Attorney General Jeff Sessions. The flustered Sessions said Senator Harris's questioning made him "nervous," and Senator John McCain hopped in to slow her down, saying that "the witness should be allowed to answer the question." It wasn't the first time Harris had been interrupted by her male colleagues, and the *New York Times* noted that Harris was the only woman of color on the Senate Intelligence Committee.

While the Senate is known for its solemnity and decorum, the interruptions of Senator Harris's line of questioning grabbed public attention, with reactions that noted racial overtones (Senator Harris is of Indian and Jamaican descent) and sexism.

Whether in Congress or in the boardroom, societal cues both blaring and subtle continue to influence how comfortable a woman feels commanding attention with her voice. If she speaks and is interrupted or her ideas are dismissed, ignored, or poached, she might decide that staying quiet is easier.

As we've seen, interruptions can pose a particular challenge for women. Perhaps in an ideal world, everyone would be allowed to complete a thought, take a cleansing breath, and focus on what's said next. But in reality, interruptions are complex expressions of multilayered social dynamics at play, including dominance, intimidation, energy, collaborative spirit. And sexism.

To insist on your right to finish your thought can feel foreign and a trespass against rules of good manners and civility. And to an extent it is, and women in particular will be penalized for breaches of decorum. We are expected, whether we like it or not, to be polite and collegial, not assertive.

When it comes to public speaking, there are a few things most people agree on: Don't use filler words. Keep it concise. Make your point, and then stop. But for women, a bit of bowing and scraping comes with the job. We're socialized to soften the impact of our statements by adding a few spoonfuls of sugar, like "Excuse me," "I'm sorry," "Do you know what I mean?," and "Does that makes sense?"—especially when speaking to a man who holds more power than we do. Linguistic codes like this put women into a double bind and make it easier for our voices to be interrupted. To appear deferential and polite, we add words. In response, we're criticized for run-on sentences that make us sound insecure. It's a no-win scenario. What's more, women have not been prepared to insist on being listened to, especially in the company of powerful men.

Owning the interruption skill set is one way for women to be heard. It's a bit like owning jumper cables: you may need them in a clutch. It won't be easy, and once you've insisted on your right to speak, there will be consequences. But this is about driving change and making space. In the meantime, feeling weird about this is a natural response, as long as you remember to forge ahead and learn how to hold the floor anyway.

As more women move into male-dominated spheres, they will inevitably change the communication culture. We're not there yet. In the meantime, human resources departments can point out the value of different communication styles that may be attached to gender the same way we are educated to value the social justice aspects of diversity in the workplace. Women sometimes ask me, Do we have to communicate like men to be heard? The answer is no.

A PBS executive told me she's modified the way she expresses herself so she doesn't have to worry about being the loudest megaphone in the room. Deanna Mackey grew up in a house where interrupting someone was the height of rudeness, so she doesn't even try to jockey for position during tense meetings. Instead, she lets the guys spout fire and fury during the meeting, then sends out an email afterward saying something along the lines of "Hey, there was so much going on at the meeting, we didn't get around to everything. Here's what I want to talk about next time." That way, she says, her ideas are on record as *hers*, and hers alone.

A confession: I like to interrupt. I love to zip in with a joke or an observation, then zip out again and listen. Understandably, not everyone enjoys that style of communication. A friend of mine used to assume the expression of a deeply disappointed lemon each time I interrupted, so I try very hard to let him finish speaking. I don't always succeed. Adaptation is healthy, and the emotional intelligence required to know when to barrel ahead and when to sit back is a skill we underestimate. Likewise, compassion and consideration are good qualities in both a human being and an employee. But until our culture makes room for all voices at the table, women should consider new tools—such as interrupting—to clear the way.

There is no foolproof recipe for a smooth interruption. But these methods will give you the template to break into conversation when the need arises, as it inevitably will. To use them well requires practice, patience, and a bracing shot of chutzpah. But given a chance, interrupting can be made much less scary and even a little bit fun. The following methods are drawn from my years on and off the radio—they're a direct response to lawmakers who barreled onward with no regard for the clock, to runaway storytellers who jumped the rails and couldn't find their way back, and to loquacious experts who needed a reminder that they were engaging in a conversation, not reciting the last act of *King Lear*. May they serve you well.

How Not to Be Interrupted

Option 1: The snapback. In a crisp gesture, hold up one finger in the general direction of the interrupter. Quickly lean forward and say, "I want to finish this thought."

IMPORTANT: *Don't look at the interrupter for more than a quick flick of the eyes; that will distract you from your thought and thus grant them the ability to continue.*

Option 2: Boardroom chicken. Continue talking, and raise the volume of your voice enough to be heard over the sound of the interrupter's voice. Do not yield until the interrupter cedes the floor. Use this technique when it matters and you need to make a point.

IMPORTANT: *You will need to practice this technique to be fully confident. Find a friend or a partner, and buddy up.*

Option 3: The nuclear option. Be direct. This is a last option for chronic interruptions that usually come from the same party. When you are interrupted, or at the first available pause, say, "Carl, you interrupted me. Let me pick up . . ."

Option 4: Engage your allies. Develop a short list of friendlies for various workplace scenarios. In this case, your ally should be on high alert: you've just been interrupted! If you're not able to hold the floor, your ally can jump in and say, "I was really interested to hear the rest of what Donna had to say." Working in pairs with a male or female ally helps ensure that your ideas see the light of day. Don't discount the guys; many men want to help, too, and might appreciate your help in return.

How to Interrupt

Option 1: The blade.

Step 1: Listen carefully. Beforehand, practice identifying "jump in" moments during meetings when you have no intention of interrupting, just to get a feel for the timing.

Step 2: Find that nanosecond of a pause or that quick intake of breath and . . . go go go! Say, "I'm going to jump in." You will need to say it quickly, crisply, and with energy. You'll also need to say it a few decibels louder than the person you are interrupting.

Step 3: Keep going! Once you're in, you're in, baby. Don't give anyone else a chance to talk once you've made the conversational cut. It will be tempting to pause in disbelief, to make sure that you actually made a good slice, but you can grab that victory lap later. Keep talking—briskly but not *too* briskly—and make your point with confidence. Congratulations, you just took the floor.

Option 2: Broken Record.

Step 1: Pick a short phrase or couple of words to use when interrupting. Again I suggest "I'm gonna jump in." In this technique, the phrase gets shortened to "I'm gonna . . ." What's important here is that the phrase is short and has the benefit of a percussive consonant, the hard *g*. Other possibilities include "Let me jump in," shortened to "Let me . . ." Find a phrase that works for you and stick with it.

Step 2: Listen carefully and pick your moment. Ready, set . . . go!

Step 3: Jump in with the phrase "I'm gonna jump in," but use only the first two words, "I'm gonna." Now repeat them over and over with increasing volume and urgency. It will sound like this: I'm gonna, I'm gonna, I'm gonna, I'MGONNAI'MGON-NAI'MGONNAI'MGONNA! This technique is essentially an audio wedge you use to drive into the conversation and create an opening. No, this is not proper English, but it's important to say it fast. No one will be worrying about your grammar, trust me.

Step 4: Keep going! You're in; this is no time to stop! You've created the opening—whatever you do, don't pause! Enjoy this feeling; you just owned the room.

NOTE: *This technique requires discipline and belief in yourself. It's also a lot of fun. Practice it on your family and loved ones! It should also come in handy at boring dinner parties.*

CHAPTER 6

This Is What a Glass Ceiling Sounds Like

On Tuesday, November 8, 2016, hundreds of visitors lined up at the Mount Hope Cemetery in Rochester, New York, where Susan B. Anthony is buried, to pay their respects. The day was fair, and the path was scattered with autumn's fading leaves. Visitors formed a kind of receiving line and didn't seem to mind waiting. They'd been coming for weeks leading up to the election, but by election day her tombstone was almost entirely covered in stickers that said "I voted." At the gravesite, the visitors placed little rocks atop Anthony's arched tombstone and touched it like a relic or posed for selfies that they posted online with

messages like "Thank you Susan for making it possible!!!"
Parents and kids came, teenagers and millennials, and women
who'd lived through the first feminist revolution.

For many there was the sense of being part of history in
the making.

These were supporters of Hillary Clinton, who had almost
made it through one of the most punishing election seasons in
recent memory. When times got rough, they wrapped themselves in the polls like a comforting electric blanket.

Now there was an air of hopeful solemnity at Mount Hope
Cemetery among Clinton's supporters. Clinton herself had
voted earlier in the day, filmed in a pantsuit of suffragette
white. The election season was almost over.

By 10 p.m. eastern time, however, Hillary's path to the
White House suddenly looked grim. She lost one battleground
state after another: Wisconsin. Pennsylvania. Michigan. Ohio.
At a certain point that night the electoral math was sucker
punching the pundits in the gut.

Early on, the only other woman in the race besides Hillary
Clinton was Republican Carly Fiorina, a former CEO of
Hewlett-Packard and eventually Ted Cruz's running mate.
Fiorina picked up momentum toward the beginning of the
primary season, only to fade away and leave the race to the
men. Perhaps because she exited early, Fiorina never attracted
the vitriol that Hillary Clinton did.

But before she became a 2017 footnote, Fiorina took a risk:

she used the occasion of announcing her commitment to run with Cruz to reference a song she'd made up for Cruz's daughters on the campaign bus. But she did more than reference the song—she sang it in front of the full complement of primary reporters, would-be voters, and, by extension, the whole of the United States. It was a surprising move, as comedian Trevor Noah pointed out later that day in more pointed terms, the kind of behind-closed-doors thing that can leave you exposed if you share it in front of a mic and thousands of people.

Say what you will: it was a risk, and Fiorina took it. She provided an authentic glimpse of who she really is. In other years, a presidential or vice presidential candidate whisper-singing a lullaby at a campaign rally would have been grounds for serious discussion. Commentators would have questioned the discipline, the judgment, and the personal gravitas of the candidate in question. The fact that the story became nothing more than grist for internet mockery means that nobody was taking Fiorina seriously anymore. Or that there was nothing at all surprising about a woman doing what we expect her to do: tending to children.

Meanwhile, all election season long, voters had been complaining that they just couldn't get a read on Hillary Clinton. Who was she really? they wondered. What was she hiding? They didn't quite trust her, although they couldn't quite say why. Was it her perfectly tailored pantsuits? Her unorthodox email preferences? Or was it maybe also something about the way she *sounded*? The adjectives describing fault with her voice multiplied: grating, scolding, shouty, screechy. Why hadn't she modified her delivery? Why did she sound like someone's grouchy old auntie sending back a BLT for having too much T and not enough B? Instead of being obsessed with Hillary's headbands, the public was now obsessed with her voice as an emblem of her flaws as a human being and candidate for office. And then she lost. The failures of Hillary Clinton were legion, as the Monday-morning quarterbacks now plainly saw, and her loss seemed obviously inevitable. The sentiment hung in the air; you had to look back and imagine that her voice had been a clue all along.

HILLARY'S VOICE, UNPACKED

It's true that Hillary Clinton's voice and demeanor have changed over the years. Kathryn Arndt was one of the early female governors of the American Bar Association, the largest voluntary organization in the world and what Arndt calls a "Southern old men's club" of lawyers and judges. Arndt remembers seeing Hillary Clinton speak in San Francisco at the ABA's Margaret Brent Luncheon to honor women lawyers of achievement.

The year was 1992, and Arndt thought the firsthand exposure to Clinton's ideas might be interesting for her conservative husband. He put up a fight, desperate to avoid being pinned to a chair while Clinton droned on for hours. But in the end Arndt prevailed. Her husband began the afternoon in hostage mode, arms crossed, expression skeptical, ready to deflect whatever was incoming. But somewhere during Clinton's address, things changed.

"She was brilliant," Arndt said. "Passionate, poised, speaking without any notes. The room was captured, including the Republicans." Her husband uncrossed his arms and leaned forward. She even saw him nodding in agreement.

"She blew us all away," Arndt added. "She was nothing at all like she was on the campaign trail in the presidential election. I don't know what happened."

Watching the video of that same speech today, Arndt still can't put her finger on the difference. Maybe it was the directness of Clinton's approach, or the passion. But in 2016, something changed. "I just didn't see the unflappable courage and conviction that I'd seen before."

Back in 1992, Clinton began her speech with a joke: "Knowing what I now know about press coverage and the like, I would bet that after all of the eloquent, moving, compelling statements we have heard, the headband is the lead story." It was a self-deprecating jab at her once famous hairstyle.

Not much changed when she ran for president twenty-three years later. But instead of her fashion choices, the public found something else to fixate on. In 2015, Megyn Kelly, then with Fox News, took an early crack at what would become a leitmotif of Wagnerian proportion: Hillary Clinton's voice. Kelly interviewed Fox's chief Washington correspondent, James Rosen, in a segment about what she characterized as Clinton's changing accent. Bloomberg had already done a feature on it, reporting on what sounded like accents that changed with the wind. Now Kelly played a clip of Clinton from 1983, when she was the wife of the newly elected governor of Arkansas. In the clip, Clinton had what seemed to be a southern drawl. She dropped her g's and sounded as though she had a pan of grits popping on the stove when she said, "The road to bein' somebody in this society starts with education."

Later on, her accent seems to lose its twang and sound more midwestern. Bloomberg Politics had an explanation: most people, especially politicians, seem to pick up a little of the local accent. And that may not be a bad thing; there's evidence that people who imitate other people may be more empathetic. But there's one thing that hasn't changed: Clinton still drops her g's no matter where she's livin' or what she's runnin' for.

Since then, Clinton's voice has launched a thousand diagnoses and think pieces. The *Atlantic* brought in a voice coach to get a handle on why people couldn't stand Clinton's voice. The verdict: Clinton pushed from her throat instead of supporting her voice with her diaphragm and finessing the air. Then again, when he was on the campaign trail, Bill Clinton's voice sounded like he'd been touring with Alice Cooper for six months. The sound of it blew way past "uncomfortable." It was *shredded*.

Patricia Finn is one of those people who could read the phone book and still have you dreamily wanting her to go on forever. Her voice is beautiful, as mellow and as rich as hand-churned butter. But she didn't always sound this way. A former vice president of global public policy at a computer software company, she made the deliberate choice to lower the pitch of her voice. "When I heard myself on tape, it wasn't the way I felt on the inside," she says. "It didn't come from a place of security."

Finn made the choice to change her voice on her own, without outside pressure. Still, she acknowledges, "For women, the cards are already stacked against you. I felt like whatever I could do to be myself but to conform to social convention . . ." She shrugs. "And voice matters."

Earlier in her career, Finn had learned the country-specific etiquette and cultural codes of communication for women and men. In one meeting with the CEO of a company in Taiwan, strict gender roles dictated that she not speak at all. Finn walked into the room and introduced herself. The CEO tipped his head toward one of the chairs ringing the conference table. Finn sat. She knew that the most powerful person in the room had to speak first, and further, she knew that person wasn't going to be her.

"It was excruciating," she remembers. After an entire half hour ticked by, during which Finn sat quietly while the CEO spoke, at last he paused and stood up. "We can work with you," he said, and ended the meeting. That was it.

Finn had succeeded by saying nothing at all. Sometimes for women, the most surefooted way to the top is to bury the voice, to be the go-along gal who doesn't mind taking the back seat. Other times it means being the hype man, or rather hype ma'am, instead of laying down the lead track, even when you know you've got the chops. There may be moments, like Finn's, when the intentional decision to be silent feels like the right choice and other moments when going dark is toxic to your sense of self.

When it comes to the question of letting your voice be heard, you have to decide on your own what you're willing to sacrifice and what winning means to you. No one should lightly surrender the right to speak.

But for women both in and out of the spotlight, there are murky waters to navigate, when surrendering your voice doesn't look like a complete silencing but instead a kind of warping, when the voice twists into an ersatz version of itself. There is no simple answer to the question, When is silence discipline, and when is it concession? Even having the most toe-curling voice won't save you from having to confront those issues for yourself.

Had Susan B. Anthony been on hand for the second presidential debate between Donald Trump and Hillary Clinton in October 2016, she might have watched a few minutes and yawned at how little had changed. In the debate, Trump alternately paced feverishly behind Clinton during her turns to speak or loomed over her within camera frame. It was notable enough that *Saturday Night Live* re-created the debate with a *Jaws*-like Trump making menacing dashes at Kate McKinnon's

Clinton as she spoke, circling wide, then suddenly lunging into close range, while scary music sawed in the background.

As a viewer, it was impossible not to watch Hillary during that debate and wonder, What must it be like to be her right now? What would I do if I were in her shoes? In her campaign memoir, *What Happened*, Clinton opened up: "It was incredibly uncomfortable. He was literally breathing down my neck. My skin crawled." The effect for Clinton was unnerving, and she toggled between the resolve to grin and bear it and to whip around and say, "Back off, creep." In the end, she gripped her microphone extra hard and opted to stay calm. On reflection, she wrote, "Maybe I have overlearned the lesson of staying calm, biting my tongue, digging my fingernails into a clenched fist. Smiling all the while, determined to present a composed face to the world."

Clinton's composed face and calm demeanor had become a potential liability. Whereas the 2016 election is known as the year that under-the-radar resentment (dubbed "whitelash" by some analysts) propelled Donald Trump to office (along with sustained acts of Russian meddling), it was also the year that cultural elements such as reality television, new-age punditry, and strands of self-expression and internet idolatry were distilled in the crucible of American culture to produce a populace that craved, above all else, authenticity and raw expression.

Against Trump's straight-shooting, non–politically correct style, Clinton looked too careful. Make that too *calculated*, said her critics. Trump looked authentic. Clinton's caution read to her detractors as a mask of duplicity and phoniness, and as the season went along, that view of her began to pick up traction. As Politico put it, "Hillary's Too Fake. Donald's Too Real." It's an interesting exercise to imagine the 1992 Clinton who spoke before the American Bar Association debating a 2016 Donald Trump. That Clinton, one imagines, might have done more than strangle her mic.

The Clinton the public has seen since the election has been more candid, acerbic, and *real* than the composed candidate on display during election 2016. If that Clinton had broken through in the second debate, it would have been a thing to see.

Kathryn Arndt, who's had lots of practice being the only woman in the room, sympathizes with Clinton.

"We always had to be measured, deliberate, and above the fray, or our credibility was damaged," she muses about her years breaking through glass ceilings as a trial lawyer. "The ravings of a less thoughtful, less educated, and less articulate guy would be heard as his birthright, and little or no consideration was given to whether he was even worth listening to."

Sounding a similar note, Patricia Finn looks back on her years as a woman in corporate America. "There are certain jobs that lend themselves to being yourself . . . Fortune 500 companies are not those places." Neither, it seems, is the world of politics.

In her introduction to *What Happened*, Clinton revealed, "In the past, for reasons I try to explain, I've often felt I had to be careful in public, like I was up on a wire without a net." It seems that after silencing herself in the service of running a disciplined, careful campaign, Clinton learned the unforgettable lesson to speak her truth even when it takes a feat of courage. "Now I'm letting my guard down," she wrote.

Ideally, all of us would act more like ourselves in any contests or campaigns we face and find a way toward *sounding* like ourselves as well. That isn't easy, but techniques like tossing a ball back and forth with a partner while you practice a speech can help dislodge a tenacious "public" voice and tip you back toward your more authentic self. Speaking from copy that's been written for the ear and not the page is also hugely effective in bringing listening audiences along for the ride.

In 2016, it's also quite possible that the weight of being a female politician running for president was a burden too heavy for one woman to carry comfortably.

There are signs that things are changing when it comes to women's voices.

Alexandria Ocasio-Cortez is a newbie in Congress, and she's already exhibiting a voice that's equal parts brains, fire, and fearlessness.

On NPR, host David Greene wanted to get a handle on

just what it was about Ocasio-Cortez that was enthralling so many people. The youngest woman to be elected to Congress, she already has a bigger Twitter following than Speaker of the House Nancy Pelosi, noted Greene before the interview with historian Rick Perlstein started.

In response to Greene's question, Perlstein called Ocasio-Cortez a transformative politician who is able to drive a message home to people, like FDR during World War II. At that Greene stopped short and said, "I just want to pause for a second because you are comparing a twenty-nine-year-old member of Congress who has literally just started her career in Congress to Franklin Delano Roosevelt." But Perlstein didn't quit there. Before the interview was over, he'd also compared her to Ronald Reagan and Winston Churchill.

The ascendency of Ocasio-Cortez may be a sign that at last we're moving beyond mothballed conversations about the sound of a woman's voice to avoid engaging directly with her ideas. In a televised primary debate broadcast on NY1, she and twenty-year Democratic incumbent Joe Crowley sparred over Crowley's position on the Immigration and Customs Enforcement agency, or ICE. Crowley admitted to calling the agency fascist, but that didn't go far enough for Ocasio-Cortez. She challenged him to call for the abolition of ICE and charged him with putting communities at risk.

The transcript conveys some of the feel of the debate, but to truly understand why the moment was a magnificent one for women, you need to see it. Gesturing with precision, Ocasio-Cortez leans across the table toward Crowley, who looks slightly ashen. Then she pounds one hand on the table, and just when you're silently mouthing the word "Whoa" to yourself and wondering if she'll dial it down a notch so she doesn't alarm her potential voters, the way you've seen women pulling back for most of your life, she pounds both hands on the table, all the while pressing Crowley commandingly on the inconsistencies of his stance and condemning him for damage done. If you're able to see the scene without the lenses you voluntarily put on that enable you to view the world as a Republican or a Democrat, you might see something like the Berlin Wall crashing to the ground for women, opening up options that were barricaded before. It's moving.

You see, when we leaf through our history books and celebrate the great orators of the past, they're always men. Posterity gave men the platform, the social capital, and the power to move hearts and minds with strong emotion. A woman who approached the arena was automatically stopped at the gates because everyone knew she wasn't what leaders sound like. Gravitas doesn't wear lipstick. So men were granted the domain of speeches that thundered and ovations that shook walls. And women became ninjas at finding the paths left unguarded. They became careful and watchful and quiet. A shouting woman was an embarrassment, not a master of rhetoric. Not every woman has a naturally forceful speaking style, but until what I fervently hope is now, this kind of unselfconscious, sustained passion has never been a viable option for a woman speaking in public.

But a young, Latina, female politician who pounded with

both hands on a table during a televised debate was elected to Congress over a twenty-year veteran. I can't wait to hear the women who come next.

When Alexandria Ocasio-Cortez was still a teenager, conservative Condoleezza Rice was one of the few women with access to the Oval Office. It was a feeling she was used to. As the first black, female secretary of state and the second African American secretary of state, she had made it a professional calling to bust through walls.

In the documentary film *Miss Representation*, Rice told the story of mounting pressure to dismantle Title IX during her tenure. "I can remember [Undersecretary of State Karen Hughes and me] going to the president and saying 'You can't do that. You don't know what it was like to be a woman in college prior to Title IX when you had to have a bake sale for your sports team to take a trip.'" Rice was in a place of influence, and she used her voice. The president listened. Title IX remained in place and is still enshrined today as a piece of legislation that almost literally helped to level the playing field for women.

"Had her voice not been there during the W. Bush administration," said Carroll University political scientist Lilly Goren, "then the W. Bush administration would likely have pursued trying to eliminate Title IX. That's one of the best sort of examples of why it's important to have women's voices at the table." Rice's story is an important reminder of why we need women's voices in places of power. The fight isn't one about territory or ego, it's about the chance to shape the world we live in.

As women push past gender boundaries in politics, they're taking their voices with them. Susan B. Anthony and other pioneers of her time squared themselves against hundreds of years of resistance to win the right for women to be active participants in civic life, to speak their minds in public. It's both a right we take for granted and one that hasn't been wholly given. Now more than ever, it's time to finish what Anthony began. Silence is not an option.

CHAPTER 7

Raising Girls to Raise the Roof

Ronald Reagan was having a hell of a time. Standing at the National Portrait Gallery in Washington, DC, one warm July day with two of my closest friends, I couldn't stop staring at his picture—one of the few photographs included in a comprehensive collection of presidential portraits dating back to George Washington. The snapshot captured Ronald Reagan and company six weeks after his inauguration at an informal moment in the Oval Office. The explanatory text says something about the photo catching Reagan doing what he did so well: telling funny stories. Reagan and the other besuited men in the crowded room were caught in the throes of laughter, midguffaw, some literally doubled over, clutching glasses of wine and little square cocktail napkins.

Every single person in the shot is male. Everyone is white. It's a room full of power brokers: future press secretary James Brady, adviser David Gergen, future attorney general Edwin Meese, vice president George H. W. Bush, chief of staff James Baker, Bud Benjamin of CBS News, and legendary news anchor Walter Cronkite.

The photo was taken in 1981, when I would have been only dimly aware of who Ronald Reagan was. Until only recently, I would have stopped in front of that photograph and my only thought would have been: That Ronald Reagan must have been quite a storyteller!

But that day in the National Portrait Gallery, the picture struck a jarring chord. The photographic evidence documenting the exclusion of women's voices, women's laughter, women's perspectives had me blinking hard, trying to contain the wrongness of the photo when it stubbornly refused to blend into the background as it once would have done. If there had been a woman in the photo, would she have been laughing, too?

I had the same reaction later that day. At the National Air and Space Museum, in the exhibit documenting the history of the United States' space program, I saw another celebration of the achievements of man after man after man. At last, as I walked deeper into the museum, there was a nod to an ill-fated space monkey and finally to the first female astronaut,

Sally Ride. It's not the Smithsonian's fault. They don't make this stuff up. It's just that the early story of American space exploration involved scores of white men, a few women, and a monkey.

Men made history; women made their lunches. When I was a girl, that was still the unremarkable wallpaper on the boundaries of my life. I couldn't have described it if I'd wanted to. Hearing only the voices of white male politicians, astronauts, scientists, religious figures, and journalists was a fact of life. It was how things were. I wondered at that moment in the National Portrait Gallery who I would be today if I had seen women participating with full voices in civic life, women talking us through the latest scientific advances, women guiding me through the day's news or the nature documentaries my family watched on PBS. I'll never know who that girl would have grown up to be.

I do know that for a time when I was young, it seemed like a good idea to grow up to be a princess.

GIRL POWER FOR SALE

Princess culture is a fact of American life. While I cut my tulle watching old-school classics like *Sleeping Beauty*, *Cinderella*, and *Snow White*, my kids grew up with next-generation Disney princess movies. They downed repeated viewings of *Mulan*, *Aladdin*, and *Frozen*, and learned the words to their favorite songs. Let's be honest, so did I. My mother tells me

I craved the color pink and remembers the time I insisted on wearing a gown made entirely of crepe paper—lovingly sewed by my grandmother for a competition—and riding on a float in a small-town parade. The gown was pink and green. I didn't take first, second, or third place.

Though as a whole, we're still figuring out how Disney's princess-powered offerings affect young minds and their nascent ideas about gender roles, we are getting a clearer picture about who in princess-land gets to do the talking.

The linguists Carmen Fought and Karen Eisenhauer took a comprehensive look at all the dialogue in Disney princess movies, from the classic era through *Frozen*, to get the big picture.

To make things easier to digest, we can divide up the movies by era. The classic movies include, you guessed it, *Snow White*, *Cinderella*, and *Sleeping Beauty*, which was released last in the bunch in 1959. After a thirty-year hiatus, the Disney Renaissance produced *The Little Mermaid*, *Beauty and the Beast*, *Aladdin*, *Pocahontas*, and *Mulan*. The Disney princess movie slumbered for another ten years, then bestirred itself again in 2009 with *The Princess and the Frog*, then *Tangled*, *Brave*, and finally *Frozen*, which was released in 2013.

What Fought and Eisenhauer found after analyzing the princess genre was startling. In the early, classic-era Disney movies, the final tally of who did most of the talking—women characters or men characters—was almost evenly split. In fact, it was the women in *Sleeping Beauty* who did the lion's share of the talking, at 71 percent. Mind you, those were movies released in the late 1930s and 1950s, so a number like 71 percent is somewhat surprising, in a good way.

Is there something manifestly creepy about all those dwarves falling in love with Snow White *while they lived together*? Sure is. Did Aurora do anything to express her agency as a person, or did she just lie down for an involuntary nap? Clearly there was a lot of catching up to do for women plotwise, but as far as sisters speaking, it was happening in these classic-era Disney movies.

Here's the rub: with the next crop of Renaissance-era Disney princess movies, something unsettling happened: women started losing their voices. Although the princesses are ostensibly the stars of this more modern generation of films, it's men who do most of the talking. Men speak 68 percent of the time in *The Little Mermaid*; 71 percent of the time in *Beauty and the Beast*; a towering 90 percent of the time in *Aladdin*; 76 percent of the time in *Pocahontas*; and 77 percent of the time in *Mulan*, who, in case you're wondering, was counted as a woman.

Surely it must get better, you might be thinking. Well, not entirely. Yes, the balance shifts back toward—and beyond—gender equity with *Brave* and *Tangled* (although it's hard not to be annoyed that the male protagonist, Flynn Rider, narrates a movie about Rapunzel), where women speak 52 and 74 percent of the time, respectively. But it's Disney's smash hit *Frozen* that leaves you shaking your head. In what seems to be a groundbreaking movie about two princesses who realize that sisterly love is way more important than any guy and a deliberate subversion of what constitutes a love story, it's the lads who have the privilege of speaking 59 percent of the movie's lines.

Taken as a whole, the study reveals worrying gaps when it comes to women's voices. We absorb what we see, especially when we're young and what we're watching comes packaged with hummable songs, princess merch, and devastating French braids. Cultural messages about the desirability of quiet women begin as a distant hum and become a deafening roar just at the time girls come of age, their antennae acutely tuned in to what their culture does and does not value about young women. In the bridge years, media empires like Disney play a part.

The marketing and consumer data platform Statista recently listed Disney as the strongest, most powerful brand in the world, and the feel-good company took in over $55 billion in revenue in 2017. With a media presence as all pervasive and flat-out powerful as that, we're faced with the troubling fact that too many of Disney's offerings are feeding the next generations of girls and boys the message that talking remains the purview of men.

Kids notice much more than we give them credit for. If we want girls to feel empowered enough to use their voices to their fullest extent, they need to see grown women doing the same. Let's be honest: in the real world, almost nobody is a princess. It's time for Disney to let women be both ordinary or royal *and* entitled to a voice. If silence can be learned, so can the power of speech.

A GENDER-NEUTRAL APPROACH

While Disney has spent decades selling children and their parents the fairy tale of billowing gowns, tiaras, and glass slippers, preschools in Sweden are striking out in a different direction. Back in 1998, the country embarked on an ongoing experiment by tasking all its public schools with the implementation of gender-neutral policies and teaching styles in an effort to get children—and someday adults—to move beyond what it calls "the limitations of stereotyped gender roles."

To that end, in some gender-neutral preschools, children aren't referred to as boys or girls but as people, friends, and sometimes "hens," a gender-neutral pronoun that was introduced in 2012. As you might expect, girls and boys in some compliant preschools in Sweden are taught that washing dishes is for everybody, tutus are just generally fun, and both tears and anger are okay, no matter what your gender identification.

At Seafarer's Preschool near Stockholm, for instance, *New York Times* reporter Ellen Barry wrote that when one- to two-year-old boys and girls were behaving as though they'd read a 1950s how-to manual, the teachers rolled up their sleeves and got to work. The boys were instructed to run the play kitchen. And the girls got to do something particularly interesting: they practiced shouting the word "No!" That part isn't too far off from what gender-neutral preschools did back in the early days, when the concept was first launched. In those days, boys and girls were separated and coached in behaviors associated with the opposite gender. For example, teachers taught girls to open the windows wide and scream.

At the end of her piece, Barry reported on a two-year-old girl who caught her teachers' attention for what they saw as stereotypically girlish behavior, like whimpering and worrying about getting dirt on her perfect pink dress. But after several months at the gender-neutral preschool, the girl was messy and rebellious at home and had become an ace at bellowing "NO!" at the top of her lungs.

Like many girls, I was quiet in class. At home, with my mother, I was someone else entirely. We would crack raucous jokes (a favorite pastime to this day), laugh, and engage in what my grandpa—usually affectionately—called hollering. Even so, teachers routinely told my mother that I was hiding my light under a barrel, and I remember concocting elaborate excuses, including sending myself to the nurse's office, to get out of speaking in front of my classmates. To this day, I could name ten talkative boys from my school years and only two or three girls. That used to be just fine, though. I didn't want to be like those boys, never shutting up, always in trouble with the teacher. I chose to be silent. That's what I hear today from other women again and again, that it's a choice to be silent, that they don't feel a need to be the center of attention.

Ask yourself: Have you ever had the feeling of being absolutely engorged with an idea you needed to voice? But instead of giving it shape and sound, you watched from the sidelines, while you told yourself that *this* might be it, the moment when you would share your mind and the idea that would turn the tide, only to watch the moment slip away forever, leaving you disappointed and caved in? I know that feeling all too well, and I can name my chosen silence for what it was: fear.

A good friend of mine, Lucy Atkinson, is a professor of advertising and public relations at the University of Texas at Austin. She's not a stand-on-a-soapbox kind of person, but whenever the media calls, she says, "I do it. I do it because I know women are so underrepresented in the media as experts in their fields. And if I can't do it for some reason, I try to recommend another woman if it's the right fit."

When Lucy snagged a guest spot on the national public radio show *On Point* and was smoothly going through the paces of that most highwire of media acts, live radio, guess who was right there with us listening to Lucy? My two kids, who were at home and are now better educated about consumer choices. Remember, we are trying to close the talking gap between men and women and to normalize the simple acts of both hearing a woman talk—especially at length—and appearing on the public stage as an expert. Kids are listening, and if they hear women experts, they will, almost through the pores of their skin, begin to imbue themselves with the idea that it's normal and expected for women to talk, that it is natural and good, and one day they will grow up to be women who talk in public spaces or honor the voices of women who do. One more time: if you identify as a woman, when someone asks you to speak—please say yes. Or better yet, volunteer.

It's not just young girls and boys who need to see women as experts, it's young women as well. Mentorship between women established in their careers and those just starting out is another ideal place to start. In a safe, trusting, and professional relationship, woman can begin conversations with one another about how they use their voices and how they might be perceived. The gulf in perceptions is surprising, and both sides may be looking for feedback.

A good rule of thumb is not to say "You sound insecure" or "You sound young" but rather "I hear an inflection that goes up at the end like a question" or "I hear that there's a loss of energy at the end of sentences." Or even "I'd like to hear your full voice." Describe the sound, not the person.

But more than that, mentors can be a leadership example; they can model confident communication and willingly engage when there's an opportunity to speak.

As far as volunteering to be an expert, you might imagine that saying yes to a request to speak is a recipe for unnecessary angst when you could just say no and spare yourself the unpleasantness of gearing up to speak in public. But it's time to get beyond the mind-set of considering ourselves the primary beneficiaries of our actions. Public speaking is just that, it is public—other people get to hear us, which is the entire point.

Where does the imperative to keep quiet come from? A study from 2004 found that girls are vastly outspoken by boys in the classroom. Boys talk nine times as often. Though teachers often coaxed a boy to speak by name, girls were often referred to in a more general way. Trinity Western University professor Allyson Jule weighed in on this.

> *We are rehearsing roles so that by the time we reach adulthood we can be even better performers of our gender. Looking at children offers insight into if women/girls are essentially quieter in public settings, or if it can be altered. My conclusion is that it can. From my research, the teacher does systematic things that can silence them. If she'd done different things, they would have said more. It's not that girls are quiet, it's that girls have been silenced.*

UNCONSCIOUS BIAS

It's a horrifying prospect to think that from the classroom on up, girls are being primed for a life of relative silence. Unconscious bias is hard to dislodge, even for the most seasoned educator. We find ourselves now at a cultural pivot point: we know that unconscious bias exists, so it's time for individuals and institutions to do some conscientious digging to seek it out and address it.

On a related note, a team of scientists recently published evidence in the *Journal of Pediatric Psychology* that we take the pain of girls less seriously than we take the pain of boys— another repellant phenomenon that no one would ever willingly admit to. And yet. Unconscious bias is just that, it's unconscious, and before we give ourselves or anyone else a get out of jail free card, it's likely a better starting position to look at our own bias instead of denying it.

The science illuminating the shape of unconscious bias is persuasive. For instance, in a randomized, double-blind study, science faculty rated male applicants for a lab manager position higher than they did female applicants, and also offered them a higher starting salary and better mentorship opportunities. In another study, college students gave their female professors lower marks than male professors teaching the same course and tended to refer to women as "teachers" while bestowing the more august title of "professor" on men.

But there may be at least one happy loophole in the struggle to rein in unconscious bias: it appears to be malleable. That means, with a little persistence, we may be able to figure out how to intervene and correct it. One early study by Nilanjana Dasgupta and Anthony Greenwald on age and race bias offers some hope. By showing study participants pictures of positive examples of black men such as Martin Luther King Jr. and Denzel Washington, for example, in contrast to other photos of roundly disliked white men like Ted Bundy and Charles

Manson (also, interestingly, Howard Stern), researchers were able to temporarily defang knee-jerk biases. We don't have a silver bullet yet, but one review of previous studies in the field of medicine found that one effective route is to train (in this case) medical personnel to see patients as individuals to help them admit their own unconscious bias. The way forward isn't obvious, but the practice of seeing people as individuals rather than representatives of a culture, ethnicity, or gender could be a commonsense starting ground. If none of this sounds very easy or comfortable, that's because it isn't. But it may be crucial to welcoming all voices to the table.

LET HER RIP

When I first began to coach women to use their voices at full capacity, I became suddenly and jarringly aware of just how steep the climb is, how baked in the cultural norms about who deserves the right to speak and the right to be heard and who should be sitting and listening. I had the conviction and zeal of a fledgling evangelist on a Sunday morning. I decided I was done silencing my daughter, who was around five years old at the time. The world would try to shut down her voice, I decided, so I would raise it from the highest mast and throw my complete approval behind her, no matter the decibel level or the social extremity.

She would wail in restaurants, declaim at the movies, and hoot wildly on airplanes. Her voice flew shining and completely unencumbered. It was glorious, unfettered, and really, really loud. For her mother, it was, at times, embarrassing. Inwardly I cringed a bit, I winced, and I ducked my head and developed a "sheepish" resting face. But even with all that, I don't think we were wrong.

Eventually, we decided to do what might be obvious in hindsight: to urge her to match her volume level to the space. If she bellows at a poetry reading, we might tell her take it down a level. But when we can, we allow her to let it rip. When girls step outside of gender norms, it's an ideal time for parents to step up.

In June 2018, Vicki Sparks became the first woman to give live, play-by-play commentary on a World Cup soccer match on British television, BBC One. The moment was a huge one for women sports commentators, who'd often heard that there was just something about a woman's voice that didn't lend itself to authoritative, exciting announcing. Sparks says her parents helped her get there by teaching her to believe in her voice.

"I was an argumentative child," Sparks tells me, "and this was generally okay with my parents. Instead of shutting me down, they tended to draw me out—challenging my perspectives, developing my opinions, entering into a debate—which helped me grow as a person." Sparks says their engagement taught her not only that it was okay to share her opinion but that her opinion was worth sharing. Argumentative girls aren't always given a path forward and room to speak. Neither are funny girls.

GET THE LAST LAUGH

The comedian Lynn Harris is working to protect her kids' voices—she has a daughter and a son. Harris is the founder of Gold Comedy, a start-up geared toward teaching girls and women the art of stand-up comedy. She's also a veteran comedian herself and an award-winning journalist and novelist.

The mission at Gold Comedy is to amplify girls' and women's voices through the act of being funny onstage. Just a girl and a mic. The company's website puts it this way: "You should try comedy because finding your funny means finding your voice and making it louder, finding your strength and making it stronger."

To be a stand-up comedian is to be alone in the spotlight, and Harris says that for girls and women, that's crucial. The tenets of improv comedy long ago filtered into the nooks and crannies of our culture, from school to corporations and non-profits, which find its team-building "Yes, and . . ." notions a fun, positive way to build productive group dynamics. That said, Harris believes that girls and women already know how to be on a team. So for them, saying "Yes, and . . ." may not be the biggest payoff. For girls and women, climbing the mountain can mean more if they do it alone.

"I love improv, I think it's great," Harris says. "But when you bring improv into a corporate setting, you're still teaching women to say 'Yes, and . . . ,' even if they don't want to." In fact, she explains, today some people, including herself, are questioning whether asking women, girls, or anyone to say "Yes, and . . ." even when they feel uncomfortable or forced can actually have a dampening effect on their personal agency.

In light of the #MeToo movement, telling a woman to say yes because it's billed as the nonnegotiable moral directive of team-building is to leave her without options. That said, clearly improv has well-defined social benefits and can help develop positive characteristics like flexibility and creativity in many people, girls and women included.

Harris agrees. "I don't mean to say these are bad values, I'm just saying they're not necessarily going to succeed in elevating women's power and respect," she elaborates. That's where stand-up comes in. "When you're getting women . . . used to being assertive alone, that's a whole different value proposition. If someone gets used to speaking onstage, being alone, talking about herself or asserting herself, it's not just this inner confidence builder. It makes her demand it next time." Put another way, she wants girls to feel *entitled* to the act of speaking alone, at length, and without being interrupted. That way, she says, those girls will go out into the world and demand the same thing again and again.

And demand it they should. Girls are up against a lot, including the epidemic of our time, the overriding pressure to be perfect, coupled with old standbys like cultural expectations to be nice, quiet, and submissive. With pressures like these, girls can grow up without a close relationship to their own voices.

TAP INTO AN AUTHENTIC VOICE

In 2003, researchers at the University of South Florida found that girls underwent incredible mental acrobatics just to answer the question, should I speak up or not? Researcher Deborah Cihonski asked girls to do the following: "Please think of a specific time when you had something important to say, but did not say it. In as much detail as possible, describe that experience." The girls Cihonski interviewed described a torturous decision-making processes that included assessment of the social cost and the potential for embarrassment and negative perception among their peers. Many of the girls opted to stay silent, a choice that, once made, becomes easier to make over and over again as life goes on.

Multiple studies show that girls begin life full of strength, confidence, and authenticity, but by the time they go through puberty their confidence ebbs away along with their voice. They split. Instead of being a unified whole, girls adopt a more innocuous persona and voice, at great personal cost. Enough research has been done in the area that it has its own designation: loss of voice.

A 2013 Boston College study showed that young women at that institution lose confidence during their undergrad years, giving themselves lower marks in confidence at the end of their four years than when they began. By comparison, young men graduate more likely to feel good about themselves even though their GPAs are generally lower than women's. And a more recent study from the University of Illinois shows that the drip, drip, drip of waning confidence may begin earlier than anyone thought. Researchers told ninety-six young children gender-neutral stories about someone who was "really really really smart" and someone who was "really really really nice," then showed them pictures of the possible main characters; two were women, and two were men. At age five, girls and boys both gravitated toward their own gender for the hyperintelligent character. But by age six, girls were much more likely to pick the pictures of men as the most likely heroes of the supersmart-person story. Imagine that: by six years old girls already doubt their own gender's capacity for brilliance.

So, yes, girls can benefit from the direct pipeline to the authentic voice that comedy can give them. "Comedy is power," according to Harris. "You get to be exactly who you are." In other words, stand-up comedy gives girls the chance to remain whole, to maintain their authentic voice or restore it, if necessary. The things girls perceive about themselves as flawed turn out to be the very things that make them funny.

"You don't have to be your best self in order to be funny. You just get to be yourself." Harris says that not only do girls get to be flawed *and* funny, they actually get to double down on those flaws and own them. Being shy can make you funny, as can being nerdy or devastatingly awkward. Harris calls it being 1.3 times yourself. And in a culture that's zapping girls' confidence starting at age six, abandoning the quest to be perfect in favor of staying themselves may very well be a hotline to preserving their voices.

When girls are up onstage, holding a microphone, everybody has to listen. This is their story, their perception, their interpretation of what's happening and what it means to them. That's power. Harris says, "You can have the loudest, most confident girl in the world, and if she gets onstage and does whatever assertive thing she wants to do and gets trolled and silenced and heckled, whose problem is that? Does she need to be more empowered? No. She's fine. We need to change how she's received." As for the confidence erosion that hits girls hard by puberty, Harris thinks the girls are all right. It's society that needs to catch up.

"Do they lose confidence because of their biochemistry, or because the whole world . . . tells them to be quiet and pretty and rewards boys for what it should reward girls for?" Harris challenges. And she's right.

All you need to do is look at the roster of highest-paid comedians in the year 2017 to answer the question, Who do we reward most for being funny, men or women? That year, Amy Schumer was the only woman to earn enough money to land a spot on *Forbes*'s list of highest-paid comedians. As for it being a glorious time for women in comedy, superstar comedian and writer Tina Fey said, "No, it's a terrible time. If you were to really look at it, the boys are still getting more money for a lot of garbage, while the ladies are hustling and doing amazing work for less." Sounds like a bleak quote from Fey's early years at Second City. But no, the year was 2016.

There's good news, though. Social progress isn't linear. It's a jagged line that moves in fits and starts, circling back upon its own footsteps, stalling out for decades, then leaping ahead out of the clear blue sky like summer lightning. As of the writing of this book, funny women are everywhere and nobody is saying otherwise.

There are Mindy Kaling, Hannah Gadsby, Tiffany Haddish, Maria Bamford, Issa Rae, and Negin Farsad. Women are funny, and so are girls—always have been. Now we must teach our daughters to value humor, make jokes, and fully participate in one of the best perks about being human: laughter. Although women are moving the needle on funny, we still face a daunting cultural climate that even today has miles to go in its slow bend toward equality.

Being funny comes with its own freedom, whether that's being the class clown, throwing down with the guys instead of cheering them on from the audience, or framing your own life story as you see it in a stand-up set. As a girl, when so little feels under your control, to own your own voice and your own stories, to take the things about yourself that you find mortifying and decide how you will think about them and integrate them into your life, is an act of revolution. When girls have equal access to power and agency, they have an ideal antidote to the slow ebbing away of self that can go hand in hand with coming of age as a young adult.

Let's encourage young women to hang on to that childhood voice, the one that unequivocally senses its right to share opinions, believe in itself, and take risks. If we're smart, we'll hold that voice close and jealously guard it, no matter how old we are or what beasts come out of the forest.

7 Ways to Raise a Girl to Raise the Roof

1. Teach her to be funny. Laugh at her jokes, and make jokes with her. Notice when she takes a shot at a joke and encourage her.

2. Celebrate talking time. Praise her when she shares her ideas, volunteers to speak in public, or takes a leadership role. Draw out her arguments.

3. Help her find a role model. Even better, be one. Show her women who share their ideas and their voices in public spaces, at home, in books, on TV, and in movies. Expose them to women who are experts in every walk of life, from microbiology to cinema.

4. If she's younger, make it a game. Give her one star for every time she asks a question, shares her opinion, or talks in public, in group gatherings, or in any space where she might be inclined to stay quiet. At five stars, buy her a puppy!

5. Open your own kennel to house and train all the puppies. Your daughter can be the spokesperson.

6. Designate Screamin' Saturdays, anything-goes days when she can holler, hoot, interrupt, and use her voice any old way she wants. Or . . .

7. Decide not to shush her anytime, anywhere, "with the possible exception of the Vatican or Wimbledon," says Lynn Harris, who stopped shushing her daughter altogether.

CHAPTER 8

What Your Mother Didn't Tell You About Your Voice

Amanda" is one of those people. Instead of nibbling at the edges of topics that matter in the reserved manner of the stoic Midwest, she plunges right in and shares the real deal. One afternoon, and you find yourself seriously considering an outing to get matching tattoos.

I first got to know Amanda when she showed up to the very first workshop I taught, and even then, she was candid. "I wasn't sure what this would be," she shared with the group, "but I just had a feeling I'd get something out of it." A few years later, and the two of us have worked and played together enough to forge a deeper bond, even if we don't see each other nearly enough. We got together on a summer's day and sat down at a coffee chain with good air-conditioning to talk.

I knew the broad outlines of her life but not all the particulars. Most of all, I knew she was very thoughtful about her voice, how she used it personally and professionally, and whether it was working in the service of her goals or not. At the time we met, Amanda was processing the last several years. She'd gotten married, become a mother, then gotten divorced.

She knew something had gone off the rails, but she wasn't sure how. She had recently separated from her husband and was struggling with her voice. It was hoarse and weak and felt strained when she tried to project it. Because of her vocal challenges, she tells me, "I'd become very disconnected from the voice that I'd had for the majority of my life."

As her marriage soured, what had once felt like a partnership marked by freedom of expression and vulnerability— mostly on her part, she realized looking back—became more guarded. On their first few dates, she remembered having a feeling of ease. She had opened up to him, shared her past and her feelings, and although he'd said less and revealed little about himself, he was, she remembered thinking at the time, a good listener.

"I thought I had a voice," she says of the relationship, pausing a moment, then adding "possibly." Later on, it became clear that the dynamic had shifted: a barbed joke here, a criticism there, until one day Amanda looked around to find that she and her husband were on very different footing: he had the big job and the jumbo paycheck, while she had opted to stay home, raise the children, and train for a new career. The criticism had become sharper and more constant, and what's more, she knew very clearly: she wasn't the one wielding the power.

"Whoa," she thought at the time, "I better watch myself."

She still talked, still asked questions, but now, there in the background, was always a note of caution.

Today Amanda's voice is far from weak. Over the past year or so, she's been working with a speech therapist who's helped her with her vocal fatigue. Our work together helped her zero in on the fact that she was forcibly driving her voice into a lower register to feel more authoritative, when it naturally fell at a slightly higher pitch. But the thing that puzzles her is that she's back at work again now in a job that calls for her to use her voice much more than she did in her past, married life. It seems odd to her that her voice would be stronger and more resilient today, when she spends hours and hours talking. Looking back now, she thinks there may have been more than a physiological reason for her hoarseness.

"I think it was a lot of fear—fear to stand up and to be strong and take my stronger part out into the world. There's a part of me that wanted to be big," she says. "To say 'I'm stepping out of that place and my voice is going to be heard.'" While it's almost certainly the case that Amanda's speech therapy helped her develop healthier vocal production, there's another truth here: fear messes with your head in ways that can affect your voice.

When we're afraid, our breath is shallow, our pitch changes, and sometimes we develop a quaver or hoarseness. Usually, vocal changes pass along with the fear, but what happens when there is chronic fear? And what about a threat of lasting fear—fear of alienating the people we love, people we want to love us, by sharing with them parts of ourselves they'd rather not hear or see, parts of us that challenge the roles we might be expected to play in a relationship?

When we're not living as our true selves with as much authenticity and integration as we can, the voice, that mirror of ourselves, can change. In Amanda's case, her voice was buried in two ways: in the hoarseness that presented itself and in the lack of regard with which it was treated in her marriage. The double whammy for Amanda meant that she wound up fighting herself and holding both her internal and external voices in check to avoid provoking her husband's ire, while at the same time experiencing the rising desire to live a bigger life and be heard. A house divided against itself cannot stand. Abraham Lincoln may have intended that sentence to apply to the union, but it holds up equally well when applied to the self.

MODERN ROMANCE

In relationships with romantic partners, women's voices are confronted with a balancing act that reflects not only the personal dynamics between the people in the partnership but how far we've come as a society in imagining what that relationship should look like and what a woman should—and should not—sound like.

Not too many years ago, my husband and I read Richard Adams's *Watership Down* aloud to the kids. Say what you will, a book about a band of brilliant male rabbits, or bucks, striking out to build a new warren free from dark influences was and always will be a page-turner. The kids were riveted. Ah, but this time around we had to stop and have a discussion about how ludicrous it was that the bucks had such a hard time explaining to the dull female rabbits what was expected of them the day they busted them free of their less-than-perfect warren. The does in the book didn't say much but seemed on board with the proposal to steal away and breed with the new, adventurous rabbits who came along. It was just a shame they were so dumb! No matter, they were willing to be mothers to the next generation of rabbits at the new colony, and that was enough.

If we view the does as stand-ins for women and the bucks for men, we have a pretty spot-on portrayal of the expectations of men and women in relationships over the last century. Men are the talkers, the planners, the actors in life, while women are there to be moved about like property; their greatest value is giving birth to babies.

That conception of gender roles was of course not invented by Richard Adams and was in fact enshrined into the nation's early coverture laws.

It took until 1966 for the US Supreme Court to formally abolish coverture, the holdover from British common law that dictated that wives and husbands were one and that one, in practice, was the man. Coverture rendered married women unable to inherit property, enter into contracts, sue, and more generally conduct business in their own name. In a legal sense, a woman ceased to exist once she was married, down to her very name, although my favorite rebel, Lucy Stone, refused to take her husband's name once she was married, giving rise to the term "Lucy Stoners"—the surprisingly cool-sounding tag for other women who made the same choice.

Without having legal standing to inherit property or make financial decisions, a woman's autonomy was chopped off at the knees and she was reduced to the status of a dependent, at the mercy of her husband or the nearest male relative in charge. (See many a Jane Austen novel.) The voice, in this case, is the right to make decisions for oneself, to have a hand in one's own destiny.

According to Princeton historian Margot Canaday, "coverture's main purpose . . . was the legal subordination of women." In 1972, it was reported that some American women could still cite coverture—or obeying their husband's orders— as a defense in court. Coverture, the cultural legacy of which is still rattling around in the attic of our collective assumptions about heterosexual marriage, was a mechanism that legally enshrined the suppression of women's agency or manifestation of voice.

Christine Whelan says that coverture may be a thing of the

past, but we still have a long way to go. Whelan is a clinical professor of research at the University of Wisconsin–Madison's School of Human Ecology. When she looks at how women are situated in their romantic relationships today, she sees a time of change, which she says makes things complicated. Though we're moving away from rigid gender norms of the past, expectations about women's voice and autonomy still loom large in the rearview mirror, and we haven't yet negotiated the new terms of engagement in romantic relationships. It's an in-between time.

"When we are in a transition period, the rules become less clear, and that puts pressure on couples and individuals to make their own rules. And making up our own rules is hard, especially if you're bucking larger social trends," Whelan told me. "So women's voices in relationships are very dependent on who they choose to partner with . . . and they're also probably dependent on how much the woman is willing to give up to be heard." That giving up of something in order to be heard is the negotiation that plays out in hetero and LGBT partnerships alike.

Life is hard. There is garbage to be taken out, bills to be paid, leaky faucets to fix, kids who need to get to piano lessons and back, and aging parents whose lawns need mowing. And although there is dignity in the running of a household and always has been, there is also the career-building phase of life that many of us go through, the looking for a job, trying to perform our best, getting promoted, and establishing a burnished professional reputation. All these things take time and energy, and the decision as to whose job it is to do them often represents a balance of the internal voice and the public voice.

This is worth a close look because, as of 2017, women still consistently perform more of the household work over a span of decades, regardless of age, race, income, or their own workloads, according to a study published in the journal *Sex Roles*. Though doing all the housework may simply be a drag in your twenties, the price tag for that same invisible work might mean that in your forties, you're the one who has less time to prepare for that big work presentation and gets passed over for a promotion as a result.

Whelan says that dynamics like these can play out in different ways and that one partner may appear to have a strong voice in a relationship, but the reality is something else entirely when it comes to the less visible, more granular decisions in a partnership.

"It can look like she's wearing the pants, but when it comes to decisions of substance—can a big purchase be made?" Whelan queries. "Why is it that she's doing everything and he's sleeping until noon? Who is ultimately responsible for the children, and who has to leave their paid employment when a child is sick? Who has to sacrifice their career for the other? Those are questions of that internal voice in a relationship that is much more muted than the public voice." It's a topic that's been on Whelan's mind.

In 2006, she published the book *Why Smart Men Marry Smart Women*. The idea was a comforting one to some single women who were concerned that their ambition and intellectual chops might keep men away. Whelan's research findings had broad appeal and even landed her an appearance on *Good Morning America*, where she used her own marriage, announced in the *New York Times*, as corroborating evidence.

But fast-forward ten years or so, and Whelan's marriage wasn't playing out the way she'd expected. Her children, she worried, were seeing a mother who lectured professionally about the importance of living with purpose but at home suppressed her own voice and goals in order to make an increasingly ill-fitting relationship work. The divide between Whelan's academic research about living a meaningful life and the blunted sense of agency she felt with her husband finally led her to seek a divorce in the summer of 2017.

"There are so many ways in which we absorb having our voice muted," Whelan says, "for the good of the larger relationship." In some cases, that trade-off pays and is part of a healthy negotiation of priorities, while in others, it leads to a rattling cognitive dissonance that can drive the voice underground.

The voice is the delta for the many incoming tributaries of self. Our many identities as partner, mother, student, daughter, professional, and friend merge and comingle, and eventually—we hope—develop into some kind of unified whole that incorporates the different aspects of our identity into one. That one self is then shared with the world via the voice and translated into our sense of agency. We live in the hope that the world will value that voice, that self, and treat it well. Sometimes our hopes are rewarded, and other times they're dashed. That's life. But when we're at war with ourselves, the physiological voice may change and reflect the conflict taking place, and our actions can become the mirror of that conflict. When that happens, we experience a literal manifestation of losing the voice. But there's also a more figurative way of going silent; we head down that road when we yield our agency to others against our own wishes, when our actions contradict our core beliefs, and when we deny our real selves when it comes to how we answer one of the biggest and most recurring question for women: whether to speak or be silent.

BEYOND THE RULES

I was in college when the frenzy over *The Rules* broke out. The best-selling book was ostensibly a no-nonsense girlfriend's guide to snagging a man, for real. I remember watching TV features on "the Rules," and absorbing lessons such as wear black nylons and your hair long, be mysterious, don't talk too much or accept Saturday dates after Wednesday, and the confusing, be a "creature unlike any other." But with all the mysterious, black-nylon-wearing nontalking you had to do to capture a man's heart, you had to wonder what happened when the megacatch you landed eventually learned you weren't a creature at all—but a human being? When he realized that he was married to an expressive, blue-jean-wearing woman who wanted to verbalize her thoughts with audible words?

The Rules may seem like an unfortunate blast from the past, but in more recent studies about what heterosexual couples desire in their partners, there's a telling nuance. Research has found that both men and women would like a partner with a sense of humor. But in a 2006 study, the psychologists Eric Bressler, Rod Martin, and Sigal Balshine found that for women, that turned out to mean they preferred a man who is funny. For men, it meant they wanted a woman who laughed at their jokes. The study didn't say whether women, in turn, would also like a partner who laughed at *their* jokes.

A University of Missouri study found the same thing in a 2015 study that had men and women "spend" money toward desired traits in a sexual partner—either the ability to tell jokes or the capacity to appreciate them. The more you spent on somebody gifted at telling jokes, for instance, the funnier the gal/guy you'd get. Turned out that men spent far more on a partner who laughed at their jokes than women did.

The Rules is no longer in vogue. But even if we aren't following directives designed to make women appear "hard to get" by deliberately smudging their personalities, we are still working overtime to figure out what goes wrong when men and women in romantic partnerships talk with each other, because even today, there is a lot that does.

WE'RE SPEAKING DIFFERENT LANGUAGES

As a growing spotlight highlights women's one-down position in the workplace and the public sphere, it's a good time to look back on what we've learned about how gender differences in communication styles impact our relationships. Georgetown University linguist Deborah Tannen wrote a slew of books on the topic, including *You Just Don't Understand: Men and Women in Conversation.* The 1990 book hit such a nerve that it spent eight years on the *New York Times* best-seller list, and Tannen reportedly heard from women who credited her with saving their marriage.

In the book, Tannen made the case that boys and girls grow up learning what she called different "genderlects," which ultimately socialize them to use communication to establish social status, reinforce personal freedom and exchange information, or build emotional rapport and establish support.

In one example from Tannen's book, a married couple is out driving and the woman turns to the man and asks, "Would you like to stop for a coffee?"

The man answers truthfully with a no. They don't stop. The woman feels annoyed because her preference wasn't considered, while the man feels frustrated because he feels the woman didn't come out and say directly what she wanted. It was just this kind of sticky wicket that Tannen waded into. Her takeaways: Women use conversation to build connections and empathy with one another, while men prefer activities and tend to use conversation as a means to establish social hierarchy and status. Women want sympathy when they bring up a story about a tough situation, said Tannen, whereas men see the story as a challenge to solve a problem. And tellingly, Tannen said, men view talk as a means to convey information and may not talk as much at home, whereas women are used to talking to convey feelings and emotions. It may surprise a woman, Tannen found, when her stoic husband goes to a party and becomes the center of attention, telling stories and jokes. When it comes to conflict, Tannen told a story about a woman who, having almost been killed when the "interesting" car her husband chose broke down, defied her husband's wishes the next time and bought a reliable but boring car instead of an interesting, less reliable one. Instead of getting angry, the husband told the wife she should have done what she wanted all along if she felt so strongly about it.

What does all this tell us about how women and men communicate? Tannen's findings, accumulated over a lifetime of research, tell us that men and women may communicate with very different intentions. With awareness and mutual good-faith negotiation, they can arrive at a compromise that's equally acceptable for both parties, or at least come to understand where problem areas lie.

But what happens when one partner's mode of communication is tipped toward greater power because it's the mode favored by society at large?

Women's consensus-building style of communication may be at odds with men's independent, hierarchy-establishing mode, if Tannen is to be believed. Asking women to negotiate a place for their voices in relationships with men is a challenge. From the self-help culture of today to the burden of pulling their countries and families out of poverty with microloans, so much is put on the backs of modern women that the time is right to look instead at the structural challenges in action even in the home and ask: How much change can we reasonably expect to make ourselves?

Zooming in on communication dynamics in the home is important because, as Christine Whelan says, "We learn to be in relationships as children, so we're . . . tied to the older generation's way of doing things." Ask yourself: What did your parents teach you about how to communicate with your partner, what did you learn by watching them, and what do you wish you could unlearn?

FORMATIVE YEARS

If women learn the worth of their voices, at least in part, by watching their mothers, then looking honestly at that joyous, painful, and marrow-deep connection must be a shortcut to understanding why we believe what we believe about them. But a funny thing happens when I ask women about their voices and their mothers: they talk about their fathers.

Not every story is a rosy one, and this observation is anecdotal—far from a replicated, academic study—but the conversations I had were compelling. When I sat down with several women to talk about what their mothers taught them about their voices, the women often had loving, thoughtful things to say. But when they really dug into the question of who shaped their relationship to their voice, it was their fathers who emerged as the main characters of the story.

Take Amanda. By and large, her mother and father had a traditional marriage. If there's one thing Amanda wished for her mother, it was that she had more *oomph*. "She grew up in the fifties. She was a woman who wanted to go to college, and her father said she couldn't because she was a girl," Amanda says. "I think she got ripped off to a certain extent and she fell into the expected—you grow up, you get married, you have children." To be clear, Amanda says, her mother is a powerful woman, but it came a bit later on in life for her. There is a slightly halting quality about Amanda as she talks about her mother; she's searching for the right words.

When Amanda talks about her father, she glows. She remembers how he was there for all his children any time of the day or night whenever they might call; how she wishes he had been around more after the divorce. At one point she remembers how he helped her through a public speaking course, how he became her sounding board, his strength powering her through. The memory is a powerful one, and she starts to cry, the only moment during our time together that she does so.

When our interview is done, Amanda says, "I feel like I should have had more to say about my mom." We talk for a while about why that is, why mothers can wind up playing second fiddle to fathers, even when it comes to their own daughters.

"She's making a lot of things happen," Amanda says of mothers in general, "but she's silent for the most part. He's the star." She remembers waiting for her father to walk through the door, the mover and shaker of the family, while her mother played a supporting role.

Anne Strainchamps grew up with a father who encouraged her voice, too. A Peabody Award–winning radio host, Anne is one of the few women I know personally who loves to command a room, and she does it well. During my decade-plus working with Anne as a producer and contributor of the nationally syndicated public radio program *To the Best of Our Knowledge*, I had ample opportunity to watch her work. I've seen her light up from the inside when an idea takes hold, challenge authority, express anger, and in general be one of the small number of women I know who would rather hold the floor than yield it.

In my life, there are certain men in my field of acquaintance— yes, they are all men—who will cause me to dive behind a produce display at the grocery store if I see them approaching. Though I like those kind, good-natured men just fine, to engage them is to commit ten minutes of my life to doing nothing more than nodding my head and listening while they do the talking.

On the other hand, these men have something rare. They like to speak, and they are unabashed about taking up space with their voices, without being troubled by the things that frequently trouble women—that they are droning on too long, that their content is boring to the listener, that they are taking too long to frame their point, or that there is spinach in their teeth while they are talking.

All this to say, Anne Strainchamps is like these men in that she loves to talk and will give herself permission to talk in public at greater length than almost any other woman I know. She is unlike those men in that, as a professional talker, she's acutely aware of her audience. Anne notices when eyes flick away, attention flags, or responses fade. If she's gotten to her point, she might stop, but if not, she'll decide consciously whether or not to keep going. Sometimes she keeps going.

Anne has the confidence those grocery store guys have but with an interviewer's awareness. Even more rare, she seems to believe she's entitled to talk, just as men are. So I was eager to hear how she wound up the way she is. When we sat down to talk, I was confident I had sniffed out her secret—her years at an all-women's college, Bryn Mawr. As it turned out, that wasn't it. At least not all of it.

"[Bryn Mawr] was my first experience living in a community where women were first-class citizens. Women came first," Strainchamps says. "I knew so many women there who were powerful and intellectual and who encouraged all of us." But Bryn Mawr's tradition of female leadership and all those portraits of female deans and presidents she walked past on a regular basis weren't the true beginning of Anne's strength of voice.

The real genesis of that relationship with her voice started with her natural propensity for talking and, notably, her formative experiences speaking around the table with her father. The memories are important enough that they're the first thing Anne wants to tell me about when we sit down together.

"I grew up in a fairly talkative house," she tells me. "I have one sister. My father was a professor and sort of a charismatic figure, and my sister and I competed for his attention." Talking and debating as they batted ideas around was the primary mode of engagement. Having a father who valued that same quality in his daughter went a long way for Anne in becoming a woman who enjoys holding forth, just like her dad.

It makes sense that in the late 1960s and '70s, when Anne and Amanda were growing up, fathers—that is to say, men—were the ones with the big careers, the ones empowered to speak and to believe in the intrinsic value of what they had to say, while women, the mothers, were more likely to play the supporting actors in the drama of family life. And supporting actors, as a matter of course, have fewer lines. It follows, then, that a father endowed with a healthy belief in his own voice would have the power to build up or damage his daughter's belief in her own voice.

"He would kind of talk, but I could always keep up," Anne tells me. "Whatever my dad was talking about—maybe French surrealist poetry—I'd go read Rimbaud and come back and say, 'Oh, the *Illuminations*, yes, it was wonderful.' I don't think there was anything he thought I couldn't do," she remembers. There was a flash and brilliance to her father that kept Anne eager to talk.

Anne's mother influenced her in a different way. "My mother has true kindness and grace and a deep moral core," she says. "If I had to put it in a phrase, I guess I'd say that my dad taught me to talk and my mom taught me to listen." But even with the rewards that go along with dazzling a room when you talk, it turns out that even Anne isn't immune from self-doubt when she commands attention and takes up space.

"This happens over and over," Anne tells me. "We have a dinner party and I'll get jazzed and excited talking to people and I'll talk a lot, I feel like ideas are sparking, and we go home and I turn to [my husband] and say, 'Did I talk too much?' I don't know when I realized, oh my God, I do this every time. . . . Why do I worry about that? I shouldn't have to ask, 'Do I talk too much?'" This dichotomy, that a woman who speaks for a living, whose ideas and propensity for expressing them are her bread and butter, should still worry whether she's taking up too much conversational real estate is telling.

One thing Anne's story demonstrates vividly is that if we wait for self-doubt to leave us entirely before we speak, we may never speak. Although self-doubt may be seen as a negative that holds women back, we may be looking at it the wrong way. That capacity to check ourselves—to verify, confirm, assess—can also be seen as a striving for verity, demonstrable evidence, and truth. If we frame self-doubt that way, it becomes an asset—as long we acknowledge the doubt, take steps to respond to it, if necessary, and move forward to speak anyway. Viewed in that way, self-doubt is the cudgel that helps to find the Venus de Milo inside the block of marble. We just need to remember to swing the ax.

Mothers, fathers, and friends can all be powerful allies when it comes to discovering the potential of our voices. And the early years at home, seeing our mothers use their voices in spheres both public and domestic, can help us think about the value of our voice and how we'd like to use our own.

But here's something else to keep in mind: when I sit down to talk with Christine Whelan about the vitriol directed toward women's voices, she says, "I bet you anything it's because of people's relationship with their mothers." So I begin a cursory exploration, not expecting to find much.

But it turns out that the internet is replete with forums, advice columns, and psychological perspectives about exactly this topic. Clearly some people really have a thing about their mother's voices. People are upset when their mothers talk, sing, yell, or interrupt, sometimes to the point of tears, skin crawling, and rage. In a way, it's to be expected. When we're living at home, under our parents' protection, someone needs to tell us what to do—take a shower, make our lunch for school, get off our phone, do our homework. All these things may well be completely contrary to what we would choose for ourselves, so we resent the intrusion on our autonomy and, by extension, the voice attached to it. There is a word for this; it's called nagging. And the nagging voice is not a voice anyone wants to hear.

Bundled with the unpleasantness of nagging are what can be deeper, embedded problems that go far beyond annoyance. We may feel our mother wasn't there for us, didn't love us, or flat-out abandoned us. She may have been abusive. These issues are triggering and may require the help of a trained therapist. But for many of us, nagging is the issue we remember from childhood and may continue to deal with as adults.

And that person reminding us to do things we'd rather not do is or was, very likely, our mother.

"Quite possibly," says Kathryn Rudlin, a therapist and the author of *Ghost Mothers: Healing from the Pain of a Mother Who Wasn't Really There*, "at an unconscious level we could be responding to negative, unresolved issues or feelings towards Mom, meaning there is likely to be a response at a level we're not aware of." In that case, she says, if we feel a negative reaction bubbling up when we feel irritated at a woman's voice, we're communicating from the past, not the present. In such situations, healing may be necessary before we can really listen.

Putting our mothers on the line for our culture's aversion to women's voices is both unfairly underestimating the impact of thousands of years of sexism and doing exactly what we're trying not to do: target women. It's also giving a nod to Sigmund Freud, which is inherently annoying and something I'd rather not do. But the idea bears some investigation. The following is a sad diagram that gets at the no-win scenario for mothers.

Society funnels women toward domestic roles like raising children → Children and young adults resent their nagging mothers → Grown-ups decide they would rather not listen to "nagging, annoying" women's voices → Society funnels women toward domestic roles like raising children

Believe it or not, asking someone to do something they'd prefer not to do is no fun, even when you hold the power and the other person does not. But *not* asking someone to do that unpleasant thing means that something important doesn't get done or that you have to do it yourself, at what is likely the end of a very long and tiring day.

Let me speak for all mothers when I say: believe it or not, we'd really rather not have to ask repeatedly for things to get done. We'd rather you all just pulled together and did them yourself without having to be asked. That way we could do the things we'd prefer to do, like think about how to solve income inequality, watch *The Handmaid's Tale*, go to the gym, or advance our thesis on pointless topology (look it up).

Think about the words leveled against women's voices in public spaces: klaxon, shrill, harsh, abrasive, hysterical, bitchy, whiny, frosty, cold. Then call your mother and tell her you're sorry. When we undervalue the role of mothers in our society and by default lay the lion's share of affirmation and praise at the feet of men, we diminish women's voices. Research shows that once women take over a field that used to be dominated by men, the pay plummets. In other words, we don't value the work of women as much as we value the same work by men. That diminishment is more than an unfortunate economic problem, it's also a problem of voice. If we value women's work in a given field, we will listen respectfully to their voices, then demonstrate that respect by paying them what men in the same field make and seeking out those women as experts as one of many indications that we value their contributions. The same is true of the labor women overwhelmingly do as parents.

Hope Edelman leads workshops for women who lost their parents when they were young. These women, Edelman tells me, long for the voices of their mothers and would love nothing more than to hear them again; it's taken them years to allow themselves to voice their grief when society has told them to hold it inside. That's a powerful reminder to love and uplift the voices of the women who brought us into the world, if we can.

Yes, our mothers told us what to do, and we will forever love, hate, resent, honor, blame, and thank them for it. But we can't take their voices from them. At the end of the day, it's all they have. It's all any of us can claim as our own.

CHAPTER 9

Building the World We Want

When we close our eyes and imagine new worlds, we aren't just escaping from the quotidian realities of our day-to-day lives; we're practicing for the future. We can arrive on that doorstep empty-handed, or we can bring our own ideas, visions, and blueprints.

What would a world in which women's voices were heard in equal proportion to men's sound like? We can look at the vanguard of equity to see possibilities dreamed into being.

There are already a few places in the world that offer us a glimpse of what lies ahead. India is one such place, where, amid serious gender discrimination, women's voices are heard at the local level in numbers far greater than they were in the past—because today they have to be.

India is a fascinating study in the use of quotas. In 1993, it set off on what the United Nations called "one of the best innovations by grassroots democracy in the world," when it approved a constitutional amendment that required village councils to reserve one-third of their seats for women. One in three villages, the mandate also said, must also have a woman council leader. The mandate rotates to another village every five years, a design that makes India a favorable testing lab for social scientists looking to isolate and measure the impact of the change.

Women in India face real and pervasive gender discrimination. According to a 2011 census, the ratio of men to women in India is 1,000 to 940, a created disparity seen largely as a direct result of the cultural preference for boys. If a fetus is identified as female, it may be aborted, while other families may keep on having children until at last they get a boy. An economic survey from 2017–18 released by the Indian government cited 63 million "missing" women and 21 million unwanted girls. Those unwanted girls may live very different lives from those of the boys around them—for instance, they may suffer from malnutrition and be allowed fewer educational opportunities. The census showed that only 65 percent of girls in India are able to read, as opposed to 85 percent of boys.

India isn't alone in mandating a required number of seats for women in lawmaking bodies. Similar quotas have originated in political parties or through national law and are currently in play around the world. Norway, Sweden, Denmark, Canada, and the United Kingdom all have quotas, as do Rwanda, Bolivia, and Cuba, all of which report greater than 50 percent representation for women. In particular, Rwanda has gone from 23 percent when the quota amendment was adopted to a female majority of more than 60 percent today.

The numbers are striking, but so is the impact. A study published in 2010 looked at eleven states in India with villages led by a woman. Researchers concluded that female village leaders were better able to bring issues women cared about to the fore and invest greater resources in education, roads, and clean water.

Significantly, they also found evidence that legislation like India's helps to clear the path for women's voices. The research, by the India Policy Forum, the Brookings Institution, and the National Council of Applied Economic Research (NCAER) of India, found that women were 25 percent more likely to speak at a village meeting if the leader of the village was a woman. In another measure of civic participation, a 2009 study found that women were more likely to throw their hat into the ring to seek elected office in a race that included both male and female candidates if the seat in question had been reserved for a woman in the previous cycle.

Maybe even more telling are findings, published in the *Quarterly Journal of Economics*, that although women in Indian villages found the transition to the quota system had been rocky, after two rounds of quotas, both male and female villagers who were initially critical of female leaders rated them at least as effective as male leaders.

As for the impact on girls, after two rounds of mandated female leaders, girls in the villages reported greater interest in working outside the home and greater levels of educational attainment.

The quota system isn't perfect. Critics say that quotas either are undemocratic because they reserve seats for women or run contrary to the principles of equal opportunity. In Rwanda, gender equity in politics brought about by government-mandated quotas has outstripped cultural change; Rwanda is number one in the world for its percentage of women in the national legislature, but in the home, women are still expected to be subservient, a reminder that shortcuts to equity like quotas may leave some important societal conversations unfinished even while structural change is being built.

Even so, case studies such as India's suggest that quotas can have a strengthening effect on women's voices and issues and clearly on their political representation, even when a parallel cultural response may take more time to develop. What's more, outcomes like India's demonstrate vividly just what can happen to outdated notions about women's leadership and the surfacing of women's voices when at last women have a voice at the table.

When entire social ecosystems witness everyday examples of female leadership, there appears to be a ripple effect. In India, this has meant that both women and men have released age-old prejudices. It has meant women speaking up and using their voices to contribute to the political process more often than they did before. For girls, it has meant the chance to seize upon greater ambition and a life that might look different from the one they saw their mothers lead. This kind of change can take generations; to see it happening before our eyes at such an accelerated pace tells us it may be time to consider quotas seriously if we hope to move women's voices toward equity.

QUOTAS IN ACTION

The state of California may agree. On September 30, 2018, Governor Jerry Brown signed a law requiring all publicly traded companies with headquarters in California to have at least one woman on their board of directors by 2019—and two women by the end of 2021. Though the law is expected to face legal hurdles, it still represents watershed legislation in the movement toward gender equity at the state level.

Cases like the successes of India and Rwanda make a compelling argument that, given the opportunity and the institutional support, women will lead and participate in political life. Even with quotas, gender inequalities won't be erased overnight across the various strata of societies, but it does mean that women could have a stronger toehold in the political system to steer toward lasting change.

As of 2017, the United States ranked 100th in a list of 190 countries when it comes to gender parity in government, according to the Inter-Parliamentary Union. Though the Nordic countries have almost achieved parity, European

countries as a whole average 24.9 percent compared to the
United States' 19.4 percent, which is itself a hefty chunk
behind the global average of 23.3 percent. That's far from a
win for a country that loves to come in first. Clearly, there's
room for improvement. In the meantime, we can move toward
equity one boardroom table at a time.

CONSTRUCTIVE CONVERSATIONS

Paula McAvoy helps people figure out how to talk con-
structively in groups. For women, that could mean taking
a stance, responding to other speakers, and learning what
it feels like to fill up time. An assistant professor of social studies
education at North Carolina State University, she worked
on the development and implementation of a training cur-
riculum for classroom facilitators called the Discussion Project
for the School of Education at UW–Madison.

The Discussion Project's goal is to help teachers and other
instructors guide their students through constructive group
conversations in which everyone participates and both students
and teachers gain the confidence and skill to engage a broad
spectrum of ideas respectfully, while recognizing that participants come from diverse backgrounds with unique personal
and cultural experiences. During times like ours, when even
simple issues can be fraught, the Discussion Project approaches
group dialogue by acknowledging that talking together about

complex topics isn't easy and isn't necessarily something students arrive on campus ready to do.

Though the program isn't expressly oriented toward making sure that women do their share of the talking, McAvoy says some of the exercises are set up to ensure that everyone participates and to help students and instructors get a feel for the right length of time to talk. For women, who may be inclined to keep it brief or keep silent, this sense of floor time could be crucial. In fact, early on in the project, even McAvoy was surprised that in discussions where she thought men and women were talking an equal amount, men were, in fact, talking more, according to an outside evaluation.

In one Discussion Project exercise, everyone is expected to talk for a minute, then hand off the floor to the next person, with a timer running for each talker. In another exercise called "The Last Word," a group of four people is given a passage to read and told to pick an excerpt with which they agree or disagree. Then the first person reads a passage and explains why they chose it. After that, the other three people in the group each get a minute to talk about why they agree or disagree and share their own interpretation. The round ends when the person who began gets one last chance to respond to the group's comment—he or she gets the last word.

Along the way, McAvoy noticed patterns about who talks and when. "If you put a question out to the whole group, men will be the first couple of comments, then women will start to participate," she reports. "I try to call on women to give the first response to try to break the trend." But talking first isn't necessarily the goal.

"It's a perfectly reasonable response to want to wait," McAvoy theorizes. Instead of teaching women to jump in sooner, "you *could* teach men to wait and see what people say." Flipping gender expectations is part of the solution in the quest to help women and men understand different conversational styles, both dominant and otherwise.

Instead of encouraging only one group of people to change how they speak and interact with others—which usually encourages women to speak more like men—we can look at what works to bring women and men onto an equal playing field and help all parties understand what it's like to be on the other side of the fence.

Here are a few exercises that groups and organizations can try to foster understanding and help even out the balance of talking time between men and women.

TIME IT

1. Run a timer during a routine, low-stakes meeting. Allow each person present to talk for no more than one minute.

2. Assign a timekeeper to set a phone alarm to go off when each person's time is up.

3. Have the leader state at the beginning of a group discussion that the participation of every person at the table is required.

4. Have the leader articulate the value of hearing from

all voices at the table and the desirability of fostering a climate that encourages everyone to speak and discourages overwhelmingly dominant speakers.

5.   Return to timed meetings once a month to create an awareness of talking patterns and inclusivity.

FLIP THE TABLES

1.   Pick a topic: coffee or tea? Then, have each person self-identify as a talker or a listener.

2.   During the discussion, have the listeners answer first and speak the longest, from one to five minutes. Limit the talkers to twenty-second responses after everyone else has spoken. The talkers are not allowed to interrupt.

3.   Discuss: What did it feel like to switch roles?

OFFER ALTERNATIVES

1.   Initiate alternative idea channels for people who don't speak as much at meetings, such as an invitation to email after the meeting with thoughts or an opportunity to participate in one-on-one meetings.

2.   Formalize "wrap-up" language at the close of each meeting to welcome the group to use these alternative idea channels. When alternative channels are used or help inform decisions, acknowledge it before the group.

If we can imagine a world in which women's voices are heard, we can build it. It's an idea the author Madeline Miller knows well. But Miller imagines worlds in reverse—she looks back thousands of years to give voice to the voiceless. In so doing, she helps us understand our own stories and how they might inform the future. Right now, Miller has turned her attention to a figure who needed more time to tell her tale than the literature of antiquity allowed her. Her name is Circe, a woman Miller calls the first witch in Western literature.

"A witch," says Miller, "is a woman who has more power than people think she should have." Sound familiar?

The world of the ancients, as passed down through the words of Ovid, Homer, Euripides, and Virgil, is a world of male perspective. Almost nothing exists of women's voices in the literature, according to Miller. They were eclipsed and silenced, deemed of little value, or never encouraged and given a channel of expression in the first place.

Miller's first novel, *Song of Achilles*, won the United Kingdom's prestigious Orange Prize for Fiction. She's a trained classicist whose writing reimagines both the stories we thought we knew and the castoffs left unexplored by history. Her specialty is reimagining some of the foundational stories of Western culture by retelling the tales of ancient mythology.

Miller's second novel, *Circe*, is an intimate exploration of voice, gender, power, and agency. As she was at work revising key scenes of the book, the #MeToo movement exploded in the news. Miller would take a break from her work, check in online, and see the stories she was writing about from hundreds of years ago played out again in the revelations about powerful men and their behavior toward women in the present day. "Being silenced, being kept from power, being abused, underestimated. All these things have been with us for a very long time," she says. "You could see them in the ancient myths, and you could see them today." The timing, for Miller, was eerie.

Although Circe played a large part in the towering stories of the ancients, her voice and perspective are notably missing. The canon's take on Circe is minimal, but she is best known as a supporting player, the goddess who turned Odysseus's men into pigs and twice assisted the hero in his tortuous quest to return to Ithaca after the Trojan War. By some accounts, Circe lived on an island with tame wolves and lions and was skilled with herbs and potions, the tools necessary for magic. To write the life of Circe, Miller scoured the available literature for clues, finally lighting on the work of Homer, who gave Miller a crucial window into who Circe was at heart when he described her as "the dread goddess who speaks like a human."

What, wondered Miller, did it mean to speak like a human? That question launched the character into a life deeply embedded in issues of the female voice. As Miller moved toward the heart of Circe's voice, she interpreted Homer's description to hint at a voice that would be nonthreatening to humans, a far cry from the deadly splendor of the gods, who could incinerate a mortal simply by appearing before her in full glory. From the start, the gods hate Circe's voice.

I asked Miller if she saw the disgust about Circe's voice as a signifier in step with the very public critique of women's voices today. "Absolutely," Miller said. "Women are subjected to a . . . holistic sense of criticism where critics feel that every part of the woman is fair game, from the way she sounds to the way she talks to her personal appearance. We criticize women in ways we would never think to criticize men . . . Woody Allen has an irritating voice, but that's considered part of his brand . . . it's a celebrated part of him. . . . For someone with an irritating voice, he's been allowed to speak and speak and speak in our culture." Not unlike Odysseus, a flawed hero from the ages, whose all-consuming epic turned everyone around him—notably women—into a sidenote.

In response, Miller made certain not to give Odysseus one chapter more than Circe got in *The Odyssey*. She flipped the script in other ways, too. For one thing, female characters are given a personality and a voice that speaks.

As a witch, speaking is important to Circe. Miller made sure of it. For a spell to work, alongside the toil, the herb gathering, the potion brewing, the single-minded intent, there is an important condition to be met. "In order to make your will manifest in the world, you have to speak it," she explains. "It's not enough to speak it in your head; you have to represent it through your voice." That same pairing of voice and intent is the match women are discovering today as they move into the power of their own voices, making evident the changes they're working to create in the world.

And far from languishing on her island, Circe revels in her newly discovered strength:

For a hundred generations, I have walked the world, drowsy and dull, idle and at my ease. Then I learned I could bend the world to my will, as a bow is bent for an arrow. I would have done that toil a thousand times to keep such power in my hands. I thought: this is how Zeus felt when he first lifted the thunderbolt.

Unless they are evil or bent on revenge, we almost never allow women to glory in their own power as Circe does. That thunderbolt is one women are looking to wield today. To hear a passage as revolutionary as this one is for women, Circe needed to speak in the first person. "I wanted to let Circe speak the whole thing," Miller confirms. "At no point did I want to move to a third-person perspective. This is a character that has been historically silenced . . . she's only there as a cameo for the male heroic tradition." Now Miller and a growing chorus are actively seeking out, listening to, and giving shape to the voices of women in fiction and beyond. It's an initiative that mirrors the world we live in today, a world suddenly listening for the voices that have been silenced.

A SUDDEN SHIFT

On October 5, 2018, I was sitting in my car in the rain, waiting for a friend to come out so we could go to dinner. Normally, I would have darted through the drops to knock on her door, but I sat riveted to my radio as NPR reported in scalding detail the *New York Times* story that changed everything: Hollywood power mogul and über-producer Harvey Weinstein had for decades been paying off multiple women, several of whom had accused him of sexual harassment. Some, the paper reported, had told reporters Megan Twohey and Jodi Kantor that they'd managed, somehow, to make it out of the hotel rooms Weinstein favored, while others had been attacked and raped. The story triggered a cultural avalanche.

In 2006, a survivor of sexual assault and abuse named Tarana Burke first coined the phrase "Me Too" as a tool to support women and girls of color dealing with sexual assault and its aftermath. In 2017, the actor Alyssa Milano used the phrase as a hashtag on Twitter and suggested, "If you've been sexually harassed or assaulted write 'me too' as a reply to this tweet." The hashtag caught fire, and survivors of sexual assault responded en masse.

Then, on November 17, members of Alianza Nacional de Campesinas published a letter in *Time* expressing their solidarity with the #MeToo movement, detailing their own stories of harassment. The letter was written on behalf of the more than 700,000 female farmworkers in the United States. The Time's Up movement followed, both in support of #MeToo and in express support of women, people of color, men, and LGBT people who might not have the public platform of other, more privileged survivors of assault or access to its legal resources.

With the rest of the country, survivors, assailants, and others alike, I watched the fires burn. Every day brought a new story to light. The men accused of sexual assault and harassment were sometimes people I'd never heard of, sometimes men whose work I admired: Sherman Alexie, James Levine, Dustin Hoffman, David Foster Wallace. At night, my husband had trouble sleeping. He'd had no idea it was like this. He asked me over and over, "Weren't you surprised?"

No, I told him. I wasn't.

I told him true stories from my own life. A male professor who dropped a condom on the floor during a female student's music lesson. A student who raped a college friend at a party and never faced repercussions. During the time I was writing this book, I heard new stories. One friend told me a story about a club manager who had told her she wouldn't be paid until she came up to his office, alone, for a birthday spanking. He tried to trap her in the room—but she was able to force her way out.

BELIEVING WOMEN

Movements like #MeToo are built on the back of storytelling. They represent motion, awareness, and the beginning of an inexorable push toward change. But their existence doesn't mean the job is done. Just this week, as I sat down to write, Bill Cosby became the first celebrity to be sentenced in a criminal trial in the era of #MeToo. Also this week, the Senate Judiciary Committee heard testimony from Dr. Christine Blasey Ford, who accused President Trump's Supreme Court nominee Brett Kavanaugh of attempted sexual assault when she was a teenager.

In the *New York Times*, the author, executive producer, and ACLU ambassador for immigration and women's rights Padma Lakshmi told the story of her rape as a teenager and sexual assault as a child. When she was seven years old, Lakshmi said, she told her mother and stepfather she'd been sexually abused by a relative. They responded by sending her to India for a year. "The lesson was," she said, "if you speak up you will be cast out." Even mothers and fathers sometimes silence survivors of sexual assault, as proxies, in a way, for the culture of silence that's been at work for ages.

At least a part of the cure is speaking. As survivors share their stories of assault and abuse, their voices are becoming strong enough to sweep away the stigma and begin to heal the shame. And if our culture learns to respond as it should, we will not minimize or degrade these voices or these stories. They need to be heard. This shared storytelling is what voices are for.

We must take our responsibility to listen seriously. If we put a finger on the scale for men before anyone says a word, instead of listening free of judgment, then we value men's voices more than women's—and we signal that men are more believable, trustworthy, and durable. In turn, women and other marginalized people will distort their voices and behaviors in order to have any kind of purchase in those male-dominated spheres. They will stifle their own voices all by themselves.

The #MeToo movement of today has created new space for women's voices. Whereas ten or twenty years ago, more survivors of sexual abuse and assault might have stayed silent, we are no longer ignoring their stories, even while we're still figuring out how to assimilate what they are telling us and how we should deal with the accused. Now that survivors are speaking in greater numbers, the world has a new, unprecedented view into the pain they've endured. With continued progress, these stories will serve a purpose: they'll encourage other survivors, catalyze change, and awaken empathy.

As the world makes way for new voices, we can welcome one another's experiences and voices. The diversity of experiences, lives, and perspectives will enrich our understanding of the world around us and help us mold a better, more inclusive future. Movements like Time's Up and #MeToo will need time to unfold. We can't rush them, and as we wait, we need to be patient with ourselves and one another as we process change and open up space for survivors to share their stories.

WHAT COMES NEXT

Change is unpredictable. It may take decades or come fast and earth-cracking all at once. Either way, we can get ready now, on the very square foot of ground where we stand.

Even when we desire a change, moving from the old to the new can be frightening and, if history is any witness, a time-tested recipe to stir up resentment and cultural blowback. With that in mind, knowing as much as we can about where we're headed can go a long way toward easing personal and cultural anxiety as we imagine a more equitable world for women and girls.

In a world with gender equity, what can we expect? For one thing, greater profitability. According to a 2015 study by the McKinsey Global Institute, if the world were to achieve complete gender parity by the year 2025, the global GDP could go up by $28 trillion. For the United States alone, the impact could be $4.3 trillion, and each state, the institute finds, would grow its GDP by a minimum of 5 percent with half showing the potential for growth over 10 percent. At the municipal level, the country's fifty largest cities could increase their GDP by 6 to 13 percent. By analyzing ten factors of gender equality in work and society, such as maternal mortality and violence against women, researchers arrived at a parity score for each state to gauge how far it has to go to reach full gender equality.

There's another compelling benefit for a society with greater numbers of women in charge: studies show that women make good decisions when the stakes are high. When I was growing up, I heard people say things like "A woman could never be president. What if she got her period and couldn't cope with tough situations on account of, you know, hormones?" Today, we know better.

Neuroscientists Mara Mather and Nichole Lighthall wanted to find out what happened to women's and men's ability to make decisions when they were under stress. So they asked their participants to dunk their hands in uncomfortably cold water—35 degrees Fahrenheit—to stress them out, then asked them to play a simple video gambling game.

Before their bodies's reaction to the frigid water increased their cortisol levels, both men and women took the same number of risks and exhibited the same decision-making processes at work. But after the stress of the water, things started to change: women made safer decisions and cashed out sooner, while men's decision-making processes took a hit—they kept playing longer and took bigger risks.

In another experiment, both genders played a card game, drawing cards from both a "safe" deck with frequent small rewards and a "risky" deck that offered up bigger but less frequent payoffs. A side-by-side comparison between the most stressed-out women and the most stressed-out men found that the stressed guys drew 21 percent more cards from the risky deck and ended up losing more overall. In general, men went for the big wins even when they weren't a great bet. In other words, in a world-going-to-hell, everyone-losing-their-minds scenario, you want a woman in the driver's seat.

A study by the University of Michigan's Stephanie Preston put participants through a diabolical test to study the same thing. She told them: Get ready, you have to give a public talk in twenty minutes. And by the way, you'll be judged on your speaking abilities. But first—play this game!

As you might expect, given the popularity of public speaking, both women and men were stressed and made poor decisions when they first began playing. But then a fascinating thing happened: the closer the timer got to the twenty-minute mark, the more women pulled it together and began to make better and better decisions. Their strategy: focusing on small, sure bets. But stressed men did the opposite: they got worse and worse at making decisions as the burden of the ticking clock wore on and, what's more, were less aware than women about how to evaluate the riskiness of their moves. How do you like them apples, Wall Street? Sadly, even though they outperformed men in the study, women rated their own strategy as poor.

Bring to mind the highest-stakes, highest-stress jobs you can. Professions like stockbroker, negotiator, fund manager, CEO, CFO, COO. The people in these positions are predominantly men. Many of them are good at their jobs and handle the demands with aplomb. But women's potential to join their ranks and excel in high-stress fields is still untapped, even though research strongly suggests that if you want someone to keep cool and steer a ship safely to harbor, you'd do well to pick a woman. We should care about this vocational opportunity gap because we care about achieving and excelling and we want our industries to perform at their peak.

Research like this isn't a complete evaluation of leadership quality and performance, but it does go a way toward allaying decades-old fears that when the chips are down, women just can't cut it. Maybe it's time to switch up our idea of just exactly who a steely eyed missile man can be. Maybe it's a woman.

As we look to the future, we can challenge ourselves to re-think our assumptions about who gets to be a hero. Heroes have everything we want for ourselves: voices, standing, respect, agency, skill, and courage. Instead of embodying the expectations of a culture that's always looking around for the perfect man to save the day, we can imagine a new hero and create a place for her to emerge, a platform for her to speak, and an audience that knows how to listen.

The world is waking up to the power of women's voices. Waking is a drowsy, back-and-forth process that involves hitting the snooze button and getting lost in delusional dreams that tell us there's no need to wake up at all. But there is hope. As women themselves come to realize the importance of their voices, they will insist upon speaking, insist upon being heard, and insist upon the value of other voices that have been pushed to the side.

Yes, change is painful, laborious, and frustrating. It helps to know all this ahead of time, so we can say to ourselves—it's supposed to be hard. Let's take a deep breath, straighten our shoulders, and talk anyway.

Conclusion

When I was a child, I loved *The Sound of Music.* I must have watched it eighty-five times on my grandparents' VCR. Remember the opening scene: Julie Andrews is up in the mountaintops of Austria with her arms flung wide? The music swells, the camera spins, and Julie Andrews spins, and then she opens her mouth and sings and it's almost the most glorious thing ever? Watching it, you feel these persistent little spikes of joy, even though you're not the one singing. Maybe you can't remember the last time you sang. That's fine. You can start where you are.

The sheer exuberance you see when Julie Andrews uses her voice—you can have that, too. You don't need to star in a Broadway musical or fly to the Swiss Alps. You can reach out to your voice, begin to use it, and explore its capabilities.

You can hum in the car, sing in the shower, speak up in the boardroom, laugh at your own jokes, ask questions when you're in the audience. Whenever possible, fling your arms wide. Say yes to that interview, yes to the talent show, yes to that keynote speech. Insist on your right to talk and your right to be listened to at work, at home, and in the public sphere. You can learn to love your voice—and, just as important, to use it.

When you do, you're working to change the world. Together, we are the voices rising, the force to mold the future, the opportunity for change.

Here's how to start. Ground zero is establishing a healthy relationship with our own voice. That begins by allowing the body—the home of the voice—to take up space and allow it the room it needs to breathe. Society will tell us to be small and quiet, but we know better. We can teach ourselves to be friends with our bellies and prepare to speak with deep, nourishing breaths that fortify and calm us. We can recognize that speaking can be challenging and scary.

As change takes root, there may be a backlash. Get ready for it; know it is coming. Keep talking.

As industries with gender imbalances seek out greater parity, women's voices will face hurdles in traditionally male-dominated places of power. Dominant modes of communication will be challenged, and new voices will face extra scrutiny until there are so many new voices that they begin to shift the culture around them. We have the language to support one another, we can amplify one another's voices, change the templates, and keep talking.

In governing bodies, the high places of power like Congress, the White House, and the Supreme Court, women's voices will reshape the political ecosystem. They'll bring with them new stories, experiences, and priorities. Women will not sound like past versions of powerful men, and they'll challenge the status quo as they go along. We can support these women on the front lines by listening when they talk and giving them a platform to speak.

We can raise girls to know that their voices matter. Instead of allowing the dominant culture to prey on their self-esteem, we can counterbalance those forces by encouraging our daughters to be funny, loud if they want to be, and vocal with their opinions and thoughts, and we can shape our institutions to support them.

We can welcome one another's stories. The diversity of experiences, lives, and perspectives will enrich our understanding and help us mold a better, more inclusive world. Movements such as Time's Up and #MeToo will need time to unfold. We can't rush them, and we need to be patient with ourselves and one another as we assimilate change and open up space for survivors to share their stories.

Your voice is precious. Honor it by using it and sending it out into the world. If you have the inclination, experiment with it. Find out what it can do—because nobody else's voice is exactly like yours. If you choose to, try speaking with a wider range, with more expression, and let your body inhabit the room it needs.

If you choose to do none of these things, that's fine, too. Your voice exists to express your own will and agency as a human being. Use it as you see fit.

There's only one thing you owe yourself and the world: keep talking.

Acknowledgments

'm deeply grateful for the help, support, and guidance that came my way during the writing of this book. A thousand and one thank-yous to Signe Pike for believing in and helping to shape *Outspoken* when it first arrived on her doorstep; to my agent, Elizabeth Kaplan, for scooping me up and going to bat for *Outspoken*; to Sofia Groopman and the team at HarperCollins for giving this book a home; to Stephanie Hitchcock for riding the waves with me on my first book and using her magic to help make the ideas sing; to Hannah Long for the savvy assistance; and to Iris McElroy, Rachel Elinsky, Penny Makras, and the production, design, marketing, and publicity teams at HarperCollins whose work amplifies the voices in *Outspoken*.

Most of all, to my family. To my mom, for coming up with

the perfect title, for the unflagging love and support, and for stepping up over and over and over again so I could write this book. You are the original outspoken voice in my life in the best possible way. To my kiddos, for understanding when I had to spend quality time alone with this book and still managing to be excited about the whole thing. I love you so much. And to my husband—fact-checker, citation sleuth, and superstar reader—who kept home and hearth running but always had time to be right by my side when I needed him during the extraordinary year that birthed this book. I could not have done it without you. Love you all beyond measure.

Thank you, Vicki Elkin, for being there to celebrate and discuss every step of the way; Elizabeth Wilson, for the constant love and support, even from far away; Louisa Kamps, for sharing your incredible literary jujitsu on deadline; Mike Klein, for the ready advice and good cheer and being the first one to jump up and down with me; Lucy Atkinson, for your sage counsel and unwavering faith in both me and the book; Jennifer Pellman, for the laughter and love from afar; Jay Amundson, for keeping the peat fire flames of friendship and creativity burning and of course the book jacket thoughts; Sarah Elmore, for the roof and snacks; Cricket Redman and her design team, for the insight and feedback; Althea Dotzour, for the patience and skill; Marika Suval, for believing in this idea from the get-go; Noriko Stevenson for sharing her love and her stories; Janelle Munns for her support and readiness to raise a glass; and Doug Gordon, for the incredible twelve-year pep talk (one day we will figure out what the government wants from the animals). My deep gratitude to Jennifer Powell, Elena Livorni, John Lucas, and Meredith McGlone.

To the Speaking While Female workshop community, thank you for sharing your stories and your voices.

Notes

INTRODUCTION

xi   I knew the Hans Christian Andersen story: Hans Christian Andersen, "The Little Mermaid," in *Andersen: The Illustrated Fairy Tales of Hans Christian Andersen* (Berlin: Little Gestalten, 2017), 55.

xii   "But if you take away": Ibid., 52.

xvi   In a study of deliberative groups: Christopher F. Karpowitz, Tali Mendelberg, and Lee Shaker, "Gender Inequality in Deliberative Participation," *American Political Science Review* 106, no. 3 (August 2012): 533–47, https://www.cambridge.org/core/journals/american -political-science-review/article/gender-inequality-in-deliberative -participation/CE7441632EB3B0BD21CC5045C7E1AF76.

xvi   Women are interrupted: Adrienne B. Hancock and Benjamin A. Rubin, "Influence of Communication Partner's Gender on Language," *Journal of Language and Social Psychology* 34, no. 1 (May 11, 2014): 46–64, https://pdfs.semanticscholar.org/f9d4/37cf7d7a60600b1154c9 c448708c0860deff.pdf.

xvi   A revealing study: Tonja Jacobi and Dylan Shweers, "Justice, Inter- rupted: The Effect of Gender, Ideology and Seniority at Supreme Court Oral Arguments," *Virginia Law Review*, Northwestern Uni- versity Pritzker School of Law, Law and Economics Research Paper

no. 17-03, March 6, 2017, 1379–1485, http://www.virginialaw review
.org/sites/virginialawreview.org/files/JacobiSchweers_Online
.pdf. The authors summarize their findings in Tonja Jacobi and
Dylan Schweers, "Female Supreme Court Justices Are Interrupted More
by Male Justices and Advocates," *Harvard Business Review*, April
11, 2017, https://hbr.org/2017/04/female-supreme-court-justices-are
-interrupted-more-by-male-justices-and-advocates.

xvi   In 2012, a Yale University study: Victoria L. Brescoll, "Who Takes
the Floor and Why: Gender, Power, and Volubility in Organizations,"
Administrative Science Quarterly 56, no. 4 (March 2012): 622–41,
http://gap.hks.harvard.edu/who-takes-floor-and-why-gender-power
-and-volubility-organizations.

xvi   women with vocal fry: Rindy C. Anderson, Casey A. Klofstad,
William J. Mayew, and Mohan Venkatachalam, "Vocal Fry May
Undermine the Success of Young Women in the Labor Market,"
PLOS One 9, no. 5 (May 28, 2014): e97506, https://journals.plos.org
/plosone/article/file?id=10.1371/journal.pone.0097506&type
=printable.

xvii male attorneys are far more likely: Commercial and Federal Litigation
Section's Task Force on Women's Initiatives, "If Not Now, When?
Achieving Equality for Women Attorneys in the Courtroom and in
ADR," New York State Bar Association, November 2017, https://
www.lacba.org/docs/default-source/committees/president%27s
-advisory-women-in-the-legal-profession/if-not-now.pdf.

xvii more than half of all law school graduates: "JD Matriculants by
Gender & Race/Ethnicity," American Bar Association, Section of Legal Education and Admissions to the Bar, Fall 2016, https://www
.americanbar.org/content/dam/aba/administrative/legal_education
_and_admissions_to_the_bar/statistics/2016_fall_jd_matriculants
_gender_race_aggregate.xlsx.

xvii In Hollywood, women spoke less: Stacy L. Smith, Mark Choueiti,
and Katherine Pieper, "Inequality in 900 Popular Films: Examining
Portrayals of Gender, Race/Ethnicity, LGBT, and Disability from
2007–2016," USC Annenberg School for Communication and Jour-
nalism, July 2017, https://annenberg.usc.edu/sites/default/files/Dr
_Stacy_L_Smith-Inequality_in_900_Popular_Films.pdf.

xvii And they were far more likely: Ibid.

CHAPTER 1: Learning to Inhale

2   Blakely became a billionaire: Lauren Drell, "Sara Blakely, Spanx: My
First Million," Huffington Post, February 13, 2011, https://www
.huffingtonpost.com/2011/02/13/sara-blakely-spanx_n_908669
.html.

3   And by the time they're seven: J. Lowes and M. Tiggemann, "Body
     Dissatisfaction, Dieting Awareness and the Impact of Parental In-
     fluence in Young Children," *British Journal of Health Psychology*
     8, pt. 2 (May 2003): 135–47, https://www.ncbi.nlm.nih.gov/pubmed
     /12804329.

3   ultimately, the science: Harriet Brown, "The Weight of the Evidence:
     It's Time to Stop Telling Fat People to Become Thin," Slate, March
     24, 2015, https://slate.com/technology/2015/03/diets-do-not-work
     -the-thin-evidence-that-losing-weight-makes-you-healthier.html.

3   mortality rates were the highest: Katherine M. Flegel, Brian K. Kit,
     and Heather Orpana, "Association of All-Cause Mortality with Over-
     weight and Obesity Using Standard Body Mass Index Categories:
     A Systematic Review and Meta-analysis," *Journal of the American
     Medical Association* 309, no. 1 (January 2, 2013): 71–82, https://jama
     network.com/journals/jama/fullarticle/1555137.

4   The garments were typically: Eleri Lynn, "Well-Rounded: A History
     of Corsetry, from Whalebone to Lycra," Slate, November 16, 2010,
     http://www.slate.com/articles/arts/gallery/2010/11/wellrounded
     .html.

4   "You should wear them": Laura Ingalls Wilder, *Little Town on the
     Prairie* (New York: Harper and Brothers, 1941), 93.

5   "It is only two months ago": *Evening Post*, September 9, 1899, quoted
     in "Charles S.'s Compendium of Cited References to Corseting in
     Era Mainstream Fashion & Some Commentary—3," http://www
     .staylace.com/textarea/charles3.htm.

5   Khloé Kardashian posted pictures: Khloé Kardashian, Instagram,
     November 4, 2016, https://www.instagram.com/p/BMzgKvPhniN/?
     utm_source=ig_embed.

6   "push your stomach contents up": Victoria Dawson Hoff, "Are Your
     Spanx Crushing Your Organs and Making You Sick?," *Elle*, January
     22, 2014, https://www.elle.com/fashion/news/a18906/spanx-shapewear
     -dangerous/.

6   Other possible, more severe maladies: Kenny Thapoung, "Celebrities
     Swear by It, but Is Waist Training Actually Healthy?," *Marie Claire*,
     March 24, 2016, https://www.marieclaire.com/health-fitness/a13489
     /celebrities-swear-by-it-but-is-waist-training-actually-healthy.

10   One of its posters read: Emma G. Fitzsimmons, "A Scourge Is
     Spreading. M.T.A.'s Cure? Dude, Close Your Legs," *New York Times*,
     December 20, 2014, https://www.nytimes.com/2014/12/21/nyregion
     /MTA-targets-manspreading-on-new-york-city-subways.html.

10   *The Oxford English Dictionary*: Katherine Connor Martin,
     "Manspreading: How New York City's MTA Popularized a Word
     Without Saying It," OUP Blog, December 12, 2015, https://blog.oup
     .com/2015/12/manspreading-word-origins.

10 "I'm not going to cross": Fitzsimmons, "A Scourge Is Spreading."

10 charging women with "she-bagging": #shebagging, Twitter, https://twitter.com/hashtag/shebagging?lang=en.

11 In Madrid's case: Ravneet Ahluwalia, "Madrid Bans Manspreading on Public Transport," *Independent*, June 8, 2017, https://www.independent.co.uk/travel/news-and-advice/mandspreading-madrid-spain-ban-public-transport-bus-metro-behaviour-etiquette-a7779041.html.

11 In the first, behavioral scientist: Tanya Vacharkulksemsuk, Emily Reit, Poruz Khambatta, et al., "Dominant, Open Nonverbal Displays Are Attractive at Zero-Acquaintance," *Proceedings of the National Academy of Sciences of the United States of America* 113, no. 15 (April 12, 2016): 4009–14, https://www.pnas.org/content/113/15/4009.

11 In the second study: Ibid.

11 The bigger (aka manspreading): Ibid.

12 the exception, of course: Susan Dominus, "When the Revolution Came for Amy Cuddy," *New York Times*, October 18, 2017, https://www.nytimes.com/2017/10/18/magazine/when-the-revolution-came-for-amy-cuddy.html.

12 new experiments failed: Dana Carney, "My Position on 'Power Poses,'" n.d., http://faculty.haas.berkeley.edu/dana_carney/pdf_My%20position%20on%20power%20poses.pdf.

21 Kay and Shipman outline the ways: Katty Kay and Claire Shipman, *The Confidence Code: The Science and Art of Self-Assurance—What Women Should Know* (New York: Harper Business, 2018).

21 Research from Northeastern University: Jukka-Pekka Onnela, Benjamin N. Waber, Alex Pentland, et al., "Using Sociometers to Quantify Social Interaction Patterns," *Nature Scientific Reports* 4, article no. 5604 (July 15, 2014), https://www.nature.com/articles/srep05604.

21 Pushing your voice like this: "Vocal Cord Lesions (Nodules, Polyps, and Cysts)," Cleveland Clinic, https://my.clevelandclinic.org/health/diseases/15424-vocal-cord-lesions-nodules-polyps-and-cysts.

CHAPTER 2: The Sound of You

26 That last part is called exhalation: "How the Lungs Work," National Heart, Lung, and Blood Institute, https://www.nhlbi.nih.gov/health-topics/how-lungs-work.

26 When we contract the diaphragm: Ibid.

29 The sound moves upward: "How the Voice Works," American Academy of Otolaryngology—Head and Neck Surgery, https://www.entnet.org/content/how-voice-works.

30   The sympathetic nervous system: "Understanding the Stress Re-
     sponse," Harvard Health Publishing, Harvard Medical School, May 1,
     2018, https://www.health.harvard.edu/staying-healthy/understanding
     -the-stress-response.

30   In fight-or-flight mode: William B. Salt II, "What Does the Sympa-
     thetic Nervous System Do?," Sharecare, https://www.sharecare.com
     /health/functions-of-the-nervous-system/what-does-sympathetic
     -nervous-system.

31   Last, and not to be overlooked: Anna Bohren, "Parasympathetic
     Nervous System: A Complete Guide," CogniFit, May 23, 2018,
     https://blog.cognifit.com/parasympathetic-nervous-system/.

31   If you stimulate: Christopher Bergland, "A Vagus Nerve Survival
     Guide to Combat Fight-or-Flight Urges," *Psychology Today*, May
     15, 2017, https://www.psychologytoday.com/us/blog/the-athletes
     -way/201705/vagus-nerve-survival-guide-combat-fight-or-flight
     -urges.

32   And with that knowledge: Xiao Ma, Zi-Qi Yue, Zhu-Qing Gong,
     et al., "The Effect of Diaphragmatic Breathing on Attention, Neg-
     ative Affect and Stress in Healthy Adults," *Frontiers in Psychology*
     8 (June 6, 2017): 874, https://www.ncbi.nlm.nih.gov/pmc/articles
     /PMC5455070/.

34   the nation's anxiety index score: "APA Public Opinion Poll—Annual
     Meeting 2018," American Psychiatric Association, March 23–25, 2018,
     https://www.psychiatry.org/newsroom/apa-public-opinion-poll
     -annual-meeting-2018.

34   a Chapman University study: "America's Top Fears 2017: Chapman
     University Survey of American Fears," Chapman University, October
     11, 2017, https://blogs.chapman.edu/wilkinson/2017/10/11/americas
     -top-fears-2017.

34   Still, the fear is so pervasive: Theo Tsaousides, "Why Are We
     Scared of Public Speaking?," *Psychology Today*, November 27, 2017,
     https://www.psychologytoday.com/us/blog/smashing-the-brain
     blocks/201711/why-are-we-scared-public-speaking.

35   During a panic attack: Lynne Harris, "Explainer: What Are Panic
     Attacks and What's Happening When We Have Them?," The Con-
     versation, March 3, 2016, http://theconversation.com/explainer-what
     -are-panic-attacks-and-whats-happening-when-we-have-them-50513.

CHAPTER 3: To Change or Not to Change?

50   The feminist author and scholar: Naomi Wolf, "Young Women, Give
     Up the Vocal Fry and Reclaim Your Strong Female Voice," *Guardian*,
     July 24, 2015, https://www.theguardian.com/commentisfree/2015
     /jul/24/vocal-fry-strong-female-voice.

50 "Dear Naomi": Debbie Cameron, "An Open Letter to Naomi Wolf: Let Women Speak How They Please," In These Times, July 27, 2015, http://inthesetimes.com/article/18241/naomi-wolf-speech-uptalk -vocal-fry.

53 According to a 2014 study: Rindy C. Anderson, Casey A. Klofstad, William J. Mayew, and Mohan Venkatachalam, "Vocal Fry May Undermine the Success of Young Women in the Labor Market," PLOS One 9, no. 5 (May 28, 2014): e97506, https://journals.plos.org /plosone/article/file?id=10.1371/journal.pone.0097506&type= printable.

56 "I can't stand it": "Sounding Off on Vocal Fry," To the Best of Our Knowledge, NPR, November 22, 2015, https://www.ttbook.org /interview/sounding-vocal-fry.

62 To some extent, surgeons: Rick Paulas, "Why Are So Many Surgeons Assholes?," Pacific Standard, July 20, 2015, https://psmag.com /social-justice/why-is-my-surgeon-acting-like-biff-from-back-to -the-future.

CHAPTER 4: Always a Bridesmaid, Never the CEO of a Fortune 500 Company

67 After reading about Margaret Thatcher's: See Bill Gardner, "From 'Shrill' Housewife to Downing Street: The Changing Voice of Margaret Thatcher," Telegraph, November 25, 2014, https://www .telegraph.co.uk/news/politics/11251919/From-shrill-housewife-to -Downing-Street-the-changing-voice-of-Margaret-Thatcher.html.

68 A mustachioed fellow: Riana Duncan, cartoon, Punch, January 8, 1988, https://punch.photoshelter.com/image/I0000eHEXGJ_wImQ.

70 "Having the right": Rebecca Solnit, "Men Still Explain Things to Me," The Nation, August 20, 2012, https://www.thenation.com/article /men-still-explain-things-me/. Her 2008 essay: Rebecca Solnit, "Best of TomDispatch: Rebecca Solnit, The Archipelago of Arrogance," TomDispatch.com, August 19, 2012, http://www.tomdispatch.com /blog/175584.

71 When women fought to participate: "Aspects of the Changing Status of New England Women, 1790–1840," Teach US History, http://www .teachushistory.org/detocqueville-visit-united-states/articles /aspects-changing-status-new-england-women.

72 The event was such a success: Joelle Million, Woman's Voice, Woman's Place: Lucy Stone and the Birth of the Woman's Rights Movement (New York: Praeger, 2003), 81.

72 In 1850, her speech: Debra Michals, ed., "Lucy Stone," National Women's History Museum, 2017, https://www.womenshistory.org /education-resources/biographies/lucy-stone.

73   Grimké went on to become: Million, *Woman's Voice, Woman's Place*, 36.

73   Her most remarkable and celebrated: "Her Words: Sojourner's Words and Music," Sojourner Truth Memorial Committee, https://sojournertruthmemorial.org/sojourner-truth/her-words.

73   Truth went on: "Sojourner Truth Biography," Biography, https://www.biography.com/people/sojourner-truth-9511284.

73   "As the poet says": Aristotle, *Politics*, 2nd ed. (Chicago: University of Chicago Press, 2013), 619.

73   "Women should remain": 1 Cor. 14:34 (New International Version).

74   When women comprise only 5 percent: Valentina Zarya, "The Share of Female CEOs in the Fortune 500 Dropped by 25% in 2018," *Fortune*, May 21, 2018, http://fortune.com/2018/05/21/women-fortune-500-2018/.

74   and both chambers of Congress: "Women in Congress 2018," Center for American Women and Politics, Eagleton Institute of Politics, Rutgers University, http://www.cawp.rutgers.edu/women-us-congress-2018.

74   "ice pick in your ear": *Glenn Beck*, CNN, March 29, 2007, http://transcripts.cnn.com/TRANSCRIPTS/0703/29/gb.01.html.

74   "No advanced step": Susan B. Anthony, "Fifty Years of Work for Woman," *Independent*, February 15, 1900.

74   "literally howled down with cries of 'Shame, shame!'": Ibid.

75   In 2011, Victoria Brescoll: Victoria L. Brescoll, "Who Takes the Floor and Why: Gender, Power, and Volubility in Organizations," *Administrative Science Quarterly* 56, no. 4 (2011): 622–41, http://gap.hks.harvard.edu/who-takes-floor-and-why-gender-power-and-volubility-organizations.

76   Her competency rating went down: Ibid.

81   "more talking": Mike Isaac and Susan Chira, "David Bonderman Resigns from Uber Board After Sexist Remark," *New York Times*, June 13, 2017, https://www.nytimes.com/2017/06/13/technology/uber-sexual-harassment-huffington-bonderman.html.

82   a study by political scientists: Christopher F. Karpowitz, Tali Mendelberg, and Lee Shaker, "Gender Inequality in Deliberative Participation," *American Political Science Review* 106, no. 3 (August 2012): 533–47, https://www.cambridge.org/core/journals/american-political-science-review/article/gender-inequality-in-deliberative-participation/CE7441632EB3B0BD21CC5045C7E1AF76.

82   Here's what they found: Ibid.

82   Follow-up analysis found: Tali Mendelberg, Christopher F. Karpowitz, and J. Baxter Oliphant, "Gender Inequality in Deliberation: Un-

packing the Black Box of Interaction," *Perspectives on Politics* 12, no. 1 (April 2014): 18–44, https://www.cambridge.org/core/journals /perspectives-on-politics/article/gender-inequality-in-deliberation -unpacking-the-black-box-of-interaction/7C72D50D31CEC1330B 58F0BDA4F9084B.

83   In 2017, women accounted for: "Women Board Director Appointments Hit Record High," Heidrick & Struggles, July 19, 2018, https:// heidrick.mediaroom.com/2018-07-19-Women-Board-Director -Appointments-Hit-Record-High.

83   Women held: "The CS Gender 3000: The Reward for Change," Credit Suisse, September 2016, https://evolveetfs.com/wp-content /uploads/2017/08/Credit-Suisse-Reward-for-Change_149566029 3279_2.pdf.

83   "When women participated more": Joe Hadfield, "Study: Deciding by Consensus Can Compensate for Group Gender Imbalances," BYU News, September 18, 2012, https://news.byu.edu/news/study-deciding -consensus-can-compensate-group-gender-imbalances.

84   When in the early days: Juliet Eilperin, "White House Women Want to Be in the Room Where It Happens," *Washington Post*, September 13, 2016, https://www.washingtonpost.com/news/powerpost/wp /2016/09/13/white-house-women-are-now-in-the-room-where-it -happens/.

87   "When we first started": "Founder of 'The Moth' Shares the Joy of Storytelling in Wisconsin," *Central Time*, Wisconsin Public Radio, April 14, 2016, https://www.wpr.org/listen/911106.

94   Only thirteen people's voices: Anahad O'Connor, "The Claim: Whispering Can Be Hazardous to Your Voice," *New York Times*, February 7, 2011, https://www.nytimes.com/2011/02/08/health /08really.html.

CHAPTER 5: Her, Interrupted

98   "Sen. Warren was giving": Amy B. Wang, "'Nevertheless She Persisted' Becomes New Battle Cry After McConnell Silences Elizabeth Warren," *Washington Post*, February 8, 2017, https://www.washingtonpost .com/news/the-fix/wp/2017/02/08/nevertheless-she-persisted -becomes-new-battle-cry-after-mcconnell-silences-elizabeth-warren /?utm_term=.7a91251ad4fc.

98   Warren went on: Katie Reilly, "Why 'Nevertheless, She Persisted' Is the Theme for This Year's Women's History Month," *Time*, March 1, 2018, http://time.com/5175901/elizabeth-warren-nevertheless-she -persisted-meaning/.

100 According to a 2014 study: Adrienne B. Hancock and Benjamin A. Rubin, "Influence of Communication Partner's Gender on Language," *Journal of Language and Social Psychology* 34, no. 1 (May 11, 2014): 46–64, https://pdfs.semanticscholar.org/f9d4/37cf7d7a60600b1154 c9c448708c0860deff.pdf.

102 "To this day": Madeleine Albright, "Madeleine Albright: My Undiplomatic Moment," *New York Times*, February 12, 2016, https://www.nytimes.com/2016/02/13/opinion/madeleine-albright-my -undiplomatic-moment.html.

103 At Northwestern University's: Tonja Jacobi and Dylan Schweers, "Justice, Interrupted: The Effect of Gender, Ideology and Seniority at Supreme Court Oral Arguments," *Virginia Law Review*, Northwestern University Pritzker School of Law, Law and Economics Research Paper no. 17-03, March 6, 2017, 1379–1485, http://www .virginialawreview.org/sites/virginialawreview.org/files/Jacobi Schweers_Online.pdf.

104 To aggravate the issue: Ibid.

105 The longer they serve: Ibid.

106 The flustered Sessions said: Michael Finnegan, "Sen. Kamala Harris Leaves Sessions 'Nervous' in Interrogations over His Refusal to Disclose Conversations with Trump," *Los Angeles Times*, June 13, 2017, https://www.latimes.com/politics/washington/la-na-essential -washington-updates-sen-kamala-harris-and-sessions-face -1497387259-htmlstory.html.

106 the only woman of color: Katie Rogers, "Kamala Harris Is (Again) Interrupted While Pressing a Senate Witness," *New York Times*, June 13, 2017, https://www.nytimes.com/2017/06/13/us/politics /kamala-harris-interrupted-jeff-sessions.html.

106 While the Senate is known: Ibid.

108 That way, she says: Author's interview with Deanna Mackey, April 21, 2016.

CHAPTER 6: This Is What a Glass Ceiling Sounds Like

113 They'd been coming for weeks: Sarah Maslin Nir, "Voters Gather at Susan B. Anthony's Grave in Rochester," *New York Times*, November 8, 2016, https://www.nytimes.com/2016/11/09/us/susan-b-anthony -grave.html.

114 At the gravesite, the visitors placed: Neha Prakash, "Tons of Women Are Putting Their 'I Voted' Stickers on Susan B. Anthony's Grave," *Allure*, November 8, 2016, https://www.allure.com/story/susan-b -anthony-grave-voting-stickers.

114 they wrapped themselves in the polls: Brian Flood, "Here's Every Major Poll That Got Donald Trump's Election Win Wrong," The Wrap, November 9, 2016, https://www.thewrap.com/every-poll -that-got-election-wrong-donald-trump.

115 she sang it: Cindy Casares, "Carly Fiorina's Singing Scored on Late-Night. But at a Rally, It Was Just Creepy," Guardian, April 28, 2016, https://www.theguardian.com/commentisfree/2016/apr/28/carly -fiorina-singing-campaign-rally-ted-cruz-vice-president-candidates -relate-to-voters.

118 there's evidence: Melissa Dahl, "Hillary Clinton Mimics Accents—But So Do You, Probably," The Cut, June 4, 2015, https://www.thecut .com/2015/06/hillary-clinton-mimics-accents-but-so-do-you .html.

118 But there's one thing: "Hillary Clinton's Accent Has Changed Vastly over the Years," Fox News Insider, April 24, 2015, https:// insider.foxnews.com/2015/04/24/watch-hillary-clintons-accent -has-changed-vastly-over-years.

118 The verdict: Clinton pushed: Daniel Lombroso and Olga Khazan, "The Science Behind Hating Hillary's Voice," Atlantic, August 1, 2016, https://www.theatlantic.com/video/index/493814/the-science -behind-hating-hillarys-voice.

121 It was notable enough: "Donald Trump vs. Hillary Clinton Town Hall Debate Cold Open," Saturday Night Live, October 16, 2016, https://www.youtube.com/watch?v=qVMW_1aZXRk&t =423s.

121 "It was incredibly uncomfortable": Hillary Rodham Clinton, What Happened (New York: Simon & Schuster, 2018), 136–37.

122 As Politico put it: David Greenberg, "Hillary's Too Fake. Donald's Too Real," Politico, July 26, 2015, https://www.politico.com/magazine /story/2015/07/donald-trump-hillary-clinton-and-the-authenticity -trap-120593.

123 "'Now I'm letting my guard down'": Clinton, What Happened, xiii–xiv.

124 bigger Twitter following: Steven Dennis, "So AOC has just passed Nancy Pelosi in Twitter followers, topping 1.85 million," Twitter, January 4, 2019, https://twitter.com/StevenTDennis/status/1081292193 690763269.

124 In response to Greene's question: "Putting Rep. Alexandria Ocasio-Cortez's Popularity into Historical Context," Morning Edition, NPR, January 22, 2019, https://www.npr.org/2019/01/22/687319721 /putting-rep-alexandria-ocasio-cortezs-popularity-into-historical -context.

124 In a televised primary debate: Amber Ferguson, "Who Is Alexandria Ocasio-Cortez?," Washington Post, June 27, 2018, https://www .washingtonpost.com/video/politics/who-is-alexandria-ocasio

-cortez/2018/06/27/daedb666-79e8-11e8-ac4e-421ef7165923_video
.html?utm_term=.4740c437f4d8.

126 "I can remember": Jennifer Siebel Newsom, director, *Miss Representation*, The Representation Project, 2011.

126 "Had her voice not": "Women Hold Few Top Posts in the Trump
Administration," *Central Time*, Wisconsin Public Radio, June 15,
2017, https://www.wpr.org/women-hold-few-top-posts-trump
-administration.

CHAPTER 7: Raising Girls to Raise the Roof

132 Carmen Fought and Karen Eisenhauser: Carmen Fought and Karen
Eisenhauer, "A Quantitative Analysis of Gendered Compliments in
Disney Princess Films," PowerPoint presentation, Linguistic Society
of America, Marriott Marquis, Washington, DC, January 17, 2016,
http://www.kareneisenhauer.org/wp-content/uploads/2016/04
/lsa-presenation-d3.pptx.

133 What Fought and Eisenhauer found: Ibid.

134 it's the lads who have: Ibid.

134 recently listed Disney: "Disney—Statistics and Facts," Statista: The
Statistics Portal, https://www.statista.com/topics/1824/disney.

135 Back in 1998: Ellen Barry, "In Sweden's Preschools, Boys Learn
to Dance and Girls Learn to Yell," *New York Times*, March 24,
2018. https://www.nytimes.com/2018/03/24/world/europe/sweden
-gender-neutral-preschools.html.

135 To that end: Ibid.

136 At the end of her piece: Ibid.

139 "We are rehearsing roles": Trinity Western University, "Boys Speak
Up, Girls Silenced in the Classroom," Newswise, June 21, 2004,
https://www.newswise.com/articles/boys-speak-up-girls-silenced
-in-the-classroom.

140 On a related note: Brian D. Earp, Joshua T. Monrad, Marianne La-
France, et al., "Gender Bias in Pediatric Pain Assessment," *Journal
of Pediatric Psychology*, (January 4, 2019), https://academic.oup
.com/jpepsy/advance-article-abstract/doi/10.1093/jpepsy/jsy104
/5273626?redirectedFrom=fulltext.

140 science faculty rated male applicants: Corinne A. Moss-Rascusin,
John F. Davidio, Victoria L. Brescoll, et al., "Science Faculty's Subtle
Gender Biases Favor Male Students," *Proceedings of the National
Academy of Sciences of the United States of America* 109, no. 41 (Octo-
ber 9, 2012): 16474–79, https://www.pnas.org/content/109/41/16474.

140 college students gave: Kristina M. W. Mitchell and Jonathan Martin, "Gender Bias in Student Evaluations," *PS: Political Science &*

Politics 51, no. 3 (July 2018): 648–52, https://www.cambridge.org /core/journals/ps-political-science-and-politics/article/gender-bias -in-student-evaluations/1224BE475C0AE75A2C2D855321 0C4E27.

141 One early study: Nilanjana Dasgupta and Anthony G. Greenwald, "On the Malleability of Automatic Attitudes: Combating Automatic Prejudice with Images of Admired and Disliked Individuals," *Journal of Personality and Social Psychology* 81, no. 5 (November 2001): 800–14, https://faculty.washington.edu/agg/pdf/Dasgupta_Gwald ._JPSP_2001.OCR.pdf.

141 one effective route: Cayla R. Teal, Anne C. Gill, Alexander R. Green, and Sonia Crandall, "Helping Medical Learners Recognise and Manage Unconscious Bias Toward Certain Patient Groups," *Medical Education* 46, no. 1 (January 2012): 80–88, https://onlinelibrary .wiley.com/doi/abs/10.1111/j.1365-2923.2011.04101.x.

142 In June 2018: Rachel McGrath, "Vicki Sparks Makes World Cup Broadcasting History (But Some People Just Cannot Handle It)," HuffPost UK, June 20, 2018, https://www.huffingtonpost.co.uk /entry/vicki-sparks-world-cup-football_uk_5b2a6e4ce4b05d6c 16c9c785.

145 In 2003, researchers at: Deborah Ann Cihonski, "The Experience of Loss of Voice in Adolescent Girls: An Existential-Phenomenological Study," thesis, University of Florida, May 22, 2003, https://scholar commons.usf.edu/cgi/viewcontent.cgi?referer=https://www.google .com/&httpsredir=1&article=2341&context=etd.

145 A 2013 Boston College study: Mary Rose Fissinger, "Female BC Students Report Lower Self-Confidence When Leaving College," *The Heights*, February 25, 2013, http://bcheights.com/2013/02/25/female -bc-students-report-lower-self-confidence-when-leaving-college/.

146 And a more recent study: Lin Bian, Sarah-Jane Leslie, and Andrei Cimpian, "Gender Stereotypes About Intellectual Ability Emerge Early and Influence Children's Interests," *Science* 355, no. 6323 (January 27, 2017): 389–91, http://science.sciencemag.org/content /355/6323/389.

147 That year, Amy Schumer: Madeline Berg, "The World's Highest-Paid Comedians 2017: Jerry Seinfeld Returns to the Top Spot," *Forbes*, July 27, 2017, https://www.forbes.com/sites/maddieberg/2017/07/27 /the-worlds-highest-paid-comedians-2017-jerry-seinfeld-returns -to-the-top-spot/#3aebaf776929.

147 "No, it's a terrible time": Mary Kaye Schilling, "Tina Fey Goes to War," *Town & Country*, March 1, 2016, https://www.townandcountrymag .com/leisure/arts-and-culture/a5146/tina-fey-interview.

CHAPTER 8: What Your Mother Didn't Tell You About Your Voice

156 Coverture rendered married women: "Women and the Law," *Women, Enterprise & Society*, Harvard Business School, 2010, https://www .library.hbs.edu/hc/wes/collections/women_law.

156 Lucy Stone, refused to take: "Lucy Stone," National Park Service, March 27, 2015, https://www.nps.gov/wori/learn/historyculture/lucy -stone.htm.

156 "coverture's main purpose": Margot Canaday, "Heterosexuality as a Legal Regime," in *The Cambridge History of Law in America*, vol. 3, *The Twentieth Century and After (1920–)*, edited by Michael Grossberg and Christopher Tomlins (Cambridge, UK: Cambridge University Press, 2008), 445.

156 In 1972, it was reported: Leah M. Persky, "Family Policymaking in the US and UK from 1960 to 2010: A Comparative Analysis of Civil Society and Legal Frameworks from a Feminist Perspective," PhD diss., University of Wisconsin–Milwaukee, 2013, 38, https://dc.uwm .edu/cgi/viewcontent.cgi?article=1149&context=etd.

158 as of 2017, women still: Rebecca M. Horne, Matthew D. Johnson, Nancy L. Galambos, and Harvey J. Krahn, "Time, Money, or Gender? Predictors of the Division of Household Labour Across Life Stages," *Sex Roles* 78, nos. 11–12 (June 2018): 731–43, https://link.springer .com/article/10.1007/s11199-017-0832-1.

159 landed her an appearance: The interview, from October 16, 2006, is preserved on Whelan's YouTube channel at https://www.youtube .com/watch?v=NqCHgp62r1I.

159 announced in the *New York Times*: "Weddings: Christine Whelan, Peter Moyers," *New York Times*, June 17, 2007, https://www.nytimes .com/2007/06/17/fashion/weddings/17whelan.html.

160 I was in college: Ellen Fein and Sherrie Schneider, *The Rules: Time-Tested Secrets for Capturing the Heart of Mr. Right* (New York: Warner Books, 1995).

161 But in a 2006 study: Eric R. Bressler, Rod A. Martin, and Sigal Balshine, "Production and Appreciation of Humor as Sexually Selected Traits," *Evolution and Human Behavior* 27, no. 2 (March 2006): 121–30, https://www.sciencedirect.com/science/article/pii /S1090513805000760.

161 Turned out that men spent: Liana S. E. Hone, William Hurwitz, and Debra Lieberman, "Sex Differences in Preferences for Humor: A Replication, Modification, and Extension," *Evolutionary Psychology*

13, no. 1 (February 2015): 167–81, https://journals.sagepub.com/doi/pdf/10.1177/147470491501300110.

162 In one example: Deborah Tannen, "Can't We Talk? (Condensed from: *You Just Don't Understand*)," https://www.dvusd.org/cms/lib011/AZ01901092/Centricity/Domain/2891/Tannen%20Cant%20We%20Talk.pdf.

163 Instead of getting angry: Ibid.

173 Research shows that once women: Asaf Levanon, Paula England, and Paul Allison, "Occupational Feminization and Pay: Assessing Causal Dynamics Using 1950–2000 U.S. Census Data," *Social Forces* 88, no. 2 (December 1, 2009): 865–91, https://academic.oup.com/sf/article-abstract/88/2/865/2235342.

CHAPTER 9: Building the World We Want

176 In 1993, it set off: Celia W. Dugger, "A Woman's Place: A Special Report; Lower-Caste Women Turn Village Rule Upside Down," *New York Times*, May 3, 1999, https://www.nytimes.com/1999/05/03/world/a-woman-s-place-a-special-report-lower-caste-women-turn-village-rule-upside-down.html.

176 According to a 2011 census: "Sex Ratio in India," Census 2011, https://www.census2011.co.in/sexratio.php.

176 If a fetus is identified: Annie Gowen, "India Has 63 Million 'Missing' Women and 21 Million Unwanted Girls, Government Says," *Washington Post*, January 29, 2018, https://www.washingtonpost.com/news/worldviews/wp/2018/01/29/india-has-63-million-missing-women-and-21-million-unwanted-girls-government-says/?utm_term=.2dcfd3019e9a.

176 The census showed that only: "Literacy in India," Census 2011, https://www.census2011.co.in/literacy.php.

177 Norway, Sweden, Denmark: "Gender Quotas Database," International Institute for Democracy and Electoral Assistance (International IDEA), https://www.idea.int/data-tools/data/gender-quotas.

177 In particular, Rwanda: Elizabeth Bennett, "Rwanda Strides Towards Gender Equality in Government," *Kennedy School Review*, August 15, 2014, http://ksr.hkspublications.org/2014/08/15/rwanda-strides-towards-gender-equality-in-government/. See also "Women in National Parliaments," Inter-Parliamentary Union, January 1, 2019, http://archive.ipu.org/wmn-e/classif.htm.

177 A study published in 2010: Lori Beaman, Esther Duflo, Rohini Pande, and Petia Topalova, "Political Reservation and Substantive Representation: Evidence from Indian Village Councils," India Policy Forum, 2010–11, 159–200, http://testnew.ncaer.org/image/userfiles

/file/IPF-Volumes/Volume%207/4_Lori%20Beaman_Esther%
20Duflo_Rohini%20Pande_Petia%20Topalova.pdf.

177 a 2009 study found: Rikhil R. Bhavnani, "Do Electoral Quotas Work
After They Are Withdrawn? Evidence from a Natural Experiment
in India," *American Political Science Review* 103, no. 1 (February
2009): 23–35, https://www.cambridge.org/core/journals/american
-political-science-review/article/do-electoral-quotas-work
-after-they-are-withdrawn-evidence-from-a-natural-experiment
-in-india/0AA2DD658A2AFE3CE30108FFCF1FDCD3.

177 Maybe even more telling: Lori Beaman, Raghabendra Chattopadh-
yay, Esther Duflo, et al., "Powerful Women: Does Exposure Reduce
Bias?," *Quarterly Journal of Economics* 124, no. 4 (2009): 1497–1540,
https://www.povertyactionlab.org/sites/default/files/publications
/310%20Female%20Quotas%20Nov%2009.pdf.

178 As for the impact on girls: Lori Beaman, Esther Duflo, Rohini Pande,
and Petia Topalova, "Female Leadership Raises Aspirations and
Educational Attainment for Girls: A Policy Experiment in India,"
Science 335, no. 6068 (February 3, 2012): 582–86, http://science
.sciencemag.org/content/335/6068/582?sid=4bd896c1-0666-4717
-977f-4f9a623316e5.

178 In Rwanda, gender equity: Gregory Warner, "It's the No. 1 Country
for Women in Politics—But Not in Daily Life," NPR, July 29, 2016,
https://www.npr.org/sections/goatsandsoda/2016/07/29/487360094
/invisibilia-no-one-thought-this-all-womans-debate-team-could
-crush-it.

179 On September 30, 2018: Jorge L. Ortiz, "California's 'Giant Step
Forward': Gender-Quotas Law Requires Women on Corporate
Boards," *USA Today*, September 30, 2018, https://www.usatoday.com
/story/news/2018/09/30/california-law-sets-gender-quotas-corporate
-boardrooms/1482883002/.

180 Though the Nordic countries have: Louise Davidson-Schmich,
"How Does the US Compare with Other Countries in Terms of
Women's Representation?," Vox, April 10, 2017, https://www.vox
.com/mischiefs-of-faction/2017/4/10/15239998/womens-representation
-congress-america.

184 Miller's first novel: Mark Brown, "Orange Prize for Fiction 2012
Goes to Madeline Miller," *Guardian*, May 30, 2012, https://www
.theguardian.com/books/2012/may/30/orange-prize-2012-madeline
-miller.

187 "For a hundred generations": Madeline Miller, *Circe* (Boston: Little,
Brown, 2018), 84.

188 the *New York Times* story: Jodi Kantor and Megan Twohey, "Harvey
Weinstein Paid Off Sexual Harassment Accusers for Decades," *New*

York Times, October 5, 2017, https://www.nytimes.com/2017/10/05/us/harvey-weinstein-harassment-allegations.html.

188 In 2006, a survivor: Abby Ohlheiser, "The Woman Behind 'Me Too' Knew the Power of the Phrase When She Created It—10 Years Ago," *Washington Post*, October 19, 2017, https://www.washingtonpost.com/news/the-intersect/wp/2017/10/19/the-woman-behind-me-too-knew-the-power-of-the-phrase-when-she-created-it-10-years-ago/.

188 In 2017, the actor Alyssa Milano: Alyssa Milano, "If you've been sexually harassed or assaulted write 'me too' as a reply to this tweet," Twitter, October 15, 2017, https://twitter.com/alyssa_milano/status/919659438700670976?lang=en.

188 Then, on November 17: "700,000 Female Farmworkers Say They Stand with Hollywood Actors Against Sexual Assault," *Time*, November 10, 2017, http://time.com/5018813/farmworkers-solidarity-hollywood-sexual-assault.

189 The Time's Up movement followed: Brittany Martin, "Here's the Story Behind Time's Up, Hollywood's Anti–Sexual Harassment Movement," *Los Angeles Magazine*, January 8, 2018, https://www.lamag.com/culturefiles/times-up-golden-globes.

190 Just this week: Laura Benshoff and Bobby Allyn, "Bill Cosby Sentenced to at Least 3 Years in State Prison for Sexual Assault," NPR, September 25, 2018, https://www.npr.org/2018/09/25/651065803/bill-cosby-sentenced-to-at-least-3-years-in-state-prison.

190 In the *New York Times*: Padma Lakshmi, "Padma Lakshmi: I Was Raped at 16 and I Kept Silent," *New York Times*, September 25, 2018, https://www.nytimes.com/2018/09/25/opinion/padma-lakshmi-sexual-assault-rape.html.

192 According to a 2015 study: Jonathan Woetzel, Anu Madgavkar, Kweilin Ellingrud, et al., *The Power of Parity: How Advancing Women's Equality Can Add $12 Trillion to Global Growth*, McKinsey Global Institute, September 2015, https://www.mckinsey.com/~/media/McKinsey/Featured%20Insights/Employment%20and%20Growth/How%20advancing%20womens%20equality%20can%20add%2012%20trillion%20to%20global%20growth/MGI%20Power%20of%20parity_Full%20report_September%202015.ashx.

192 For the United States alone: Kweilin Ellingrud, Anu Madgavkar, James Manyika, et al., *The Power of Parity: Advancing Women's Equality in the United States*, McKinsey Global Institute, April 2016, https://www.mckinsey.com/~/media/McKinsey/Featured%20Insights/Employment%20and%20Growth/The%20power%20of%20parity%20Advancing%20womens%20equality%20in%20the%20United%20States/MGI-Power-of-Parity-in-US-Full-report-April-2016.ashx.

193 Neuroscientists Mara Mather and Nichole Lighthall: Mara Mather and
     Nichole R. Lighthall, "Risk and Reward Are Processed Differently
     in Decisions Made Under Stress," *Current Directions in Psycholog-
     ical Science* 21, no. 1 (February 21, 2012): 36–41, https://journals
     .sagepub.com/doi/abs/10.1177/0963721411429452. See also Therese
     Huston, "Are Women Better Decision Makers?," *New York Times*,
     October 17, 2014, https://www.nytimes.com/2014/10/19/opinion
     /sunday/are-women-better-decision-makers.html.

194 A study by the University: S. D. Preston, T. W. Buchanan, R. B.
     Stansfield, and A. Bechara, "Effects of Anticipatory Stress on Decision
     Making in a Gambling Task," *Behavioral Neuroscience* 121, no. 2
     (April 2007): 257–63, https://pdfs.semanticscholar.org/c532/aed33f5
     a7e004aa68421d112a39740a863bb.pdf.

Index

About the Author

VERONICA RUECKERT is a Peabody Award–winning communications specialist. She was the cohost of Wisconsin Public Radio's statewide news magazine *Central Time* and hosted the statewide call-in program *The Veronica Rueckert Show*. Earlier, she worked as a senior producer and contributor on the national program *To the Best of Our Knowledge*, distributed by Public Radio International. Her essays have aired to national audiences via NPR and PRI. She conducts media training and national media outreach at the University of Wisconsin–Madison.

Veronica holds a degree in vocal performance and specializes in teaching people how to work with their speaking voice as an instrument of self-expression and uncover its innate potential, persuasive power, and inherent strength. She leads workshops, delivers keynotes, and coaches clients at Veronica Rueckert Coaching.